CAMBRIDGE

C1
ADVANCED 5

WITHOUT ANSWERS

AUTHENTIC PRACTICE TESTS

 WITH AUDIO

CAMBRIDGE
UNIVERSITY PRESS & ASSESSMENT

Shaftesbury Road, Cambridge CB2 8EA, United Kingdom

One Liberty Plaza, 20th Floor, New York, NY 10006, USA

477 Williamstown Road, Port Melbourne, VIC 3207, Australia

314–321, 3rd Floor, Plot 3, Splendor Forum, Jasola District Centre, New Delhi – 110025, India

103 Penang Road, #05–06/07, Visioncrest Commercial, Singapore 238467

Cambridge University Press & Assessment is a department of the University of Cambridge.

We share the University's mission to contribute to society through the pursuit of education, learning and research at the highest international levels of excellence.

www.cambridge.org
Information on this title: www.cambridge.org/9781009808873

© Cambridge University Press & Assessment 2025

First published 2025

20 19 18 17 16 15 14 13 12 11 10 9 8 7 6 5 4 3 2 1

Printed in the Netherlands by Wilco BV

A catalogue record for this publication is available from the British Library

ISBN 978-1-009-80886-6 Student's Book with Answers with Audio with Resource Bank
ISBN 978-1-009-80887-3 Student's Book without Answers with Audio

Contents

Introduction

Prepare for the exam with practice tests from Cambridge

Inside you'll find four authentic examination papers from Cambridge English. They are the perfect way to practise – EXACTLY like the real exam.

Why are they unique?

All our authentic practice tests go through the same design process as the *C1 Advanced* exam. We check every single part of our practice tests with real students under exam conditions, to make sure we give you the most authentic experience possible.

Students can practise these tests on their own or with the help of a teacher to familiarise themselves with the exam format, understand the scoring system and practise exam technique.

Cambridge English Qualifications	CEFR Level	UK National Qualifications
C2 Proficiency	C2	3
C1 Advanced	C1	2
B2 First	B2	1
B1 Preliminary	B1	Entry 3
A2 Key	A2	Entry 2

Further information

The information contained in this practice book is designed to be an overview of the exam. For a full description of all of the above exams, including information about task types, testing focus and preparation, please see the relevant handbooks which can be obtained from the Cambridge University Press & Assessment English website at: **cambridgeenglish.org**.

The structure of *C1 Advanced:* an overview

The *Cambridge English Qualifications C1 Advanced* examination consists of four papers:

Reading and Use of English: 1 hour 30 minutes
Candidates need to be able to understand texts from publications such as fiction and non-fiction books, journals, newspapers and magazines.

Writing: 1 hour 30 minutes
Candidates have to show that they can produce two different pieces of writing: a compulsory essay in Part 1, and one from a choice of three tasks in Part 2.

Listening: 40 minutes approximately
Candidates need to show they can understand the meaning of a range of spoken material, including lectures, radio broadcasts, speeches and talks.

Speaking: 15 minutes (or 21 minutes for groups of 3)
Candidates take the Speaking test with another candidate or in a group of three, and are tested on their ability to take part in different types of interaction: with the examiner, with the other candidate and by themselves.

	Overall length	Number of tasks/parts	Number of items
Reading and Use of English	1 hour and 30 minutes	8	56
Writing	1 hour and 30 minutes	2	2
Listening	Approx. 40 mins	4	30
Speaking	15 mins	4	-
Total	3 hours and 55 mins approx.		

Grading

All candidates receive a Statement of Results. Candidates whose performance ranges between CEFR Levels B2 and C2 (Cambridge English Scale scores of 160–210) also receive a certificate.

- Candidates who achieve **Grade A** (Cambridge English Scale scores of 200–210) receive the Certificate in Advanced English stating that they demonstrated ability at Level C2.

- Candidates who achieve **Grade B** or **C** (Cambridge English Scale scores of 180–199) receive the Certificate in Advanced English at Level C1.

- Candidates whose performance is below Level C1, but falls within **Level B2** (Cambridge English Scale scores of 160–179), receive a Cambridge English certificate stating that they demonstrated ability at Level B2.

For further information on grading and results, please see the Cambridge University Press & Assessment English website at: **cambridgeenglish.org**.

Speaking: an overview for candidates

You take the Speaking test with another candidate (possibly two candidates), referred to here as your partner. There are two examiners. One will speak to you and your partner, and the other will be listening. Both examiners will award marks.

Part 1 (2 minutes)

The examiner asks you and your partner questions about yourselves, and then moves onto wider questions about your life: for example, your leisure activities, studies, travel and daily routine. You are expected to respond to the examiner's questions and listen to what your partner has to say.

Part 2 (4 minutes)

In this part, you are given the opportunity to talk on your own for one minute. The examiner gives you a set of three pictures and a question. The examiner will ask you to talk about two of the pictures in response to the question for about one minute. It is important to listen carefully to the examiner's instructions. The examiner then asks your partner a question about your pictures and your partner responds briefly.

Your partner will then be given another set of pictures to look at. Your partner talks about these pictures for one minute. This time the examiner asks you a question about your partner's pictures and you respond briefly.

Part 3 (4 minutes)

In this part of the test, you and your partner are asked to talk together. The examiner places a question and some text prompts on the table between you. These prompts provide the basis for the first discussion.

After this discussion, the examiner will give you another task where you are asked to make a decision on the topic.

Part 4 (5 minutes)

The examiner asks you and your partner some further questions about the topics you have discussed in Part 3. You may be asked to respond to the examiner's questions on your own, or in discussion with your partner.

Test 1

Icon	What does it mean?
🔊	Listening test audio (Scan the QR code or download from the Resource Bank)

Test 1

READING AND USE OF ENGLISH (1 hour 30 minutes)

Part 1

For questions **1–8**, read the text below and decide which answer (**A, B, C** or **D**) best fits each gap. There is an example at the beginning (**0**).

Mark your answers **on the separate answer sheet**.

Example:

0   A active   **B** vigorous   **C** forceful   **D** alert

0	A ●	B ○	C ○	D ○

Welcome to Mars

Mauna Loa in Hawaii is among the world's most **(0)** .... volcanoes. However, according to NASA (the National Aeronautics and Space Administration), this **(1)** .... spot is ideal for **(2)** .... a space mission to Mars. Six scientists were therefore housed near the volcano in a small white dome for an 8-month experiment, the **(3)** .... of which was to **(4)** .... information on how lengthy Mars missions could psychologically affect astronauts. The six scientists closed themselves off from the world in order to undertake studies into the demands of life on Mars. Their task was to see how isolation and the lack of privacy affect social **(5)** .... of would-be explorers' lives.

Conditions on Mars are tough, so the six had to manage without many of life's **(6)** .... , like fresh fruit and unlimited water. They only left the dome once a week to **(7)** .... field studies in the volcanic crater, wearing suits similar to those being designed for Mars astronauts.

The research findings are expected to have considerable **(8)** .... on NASA's decisions when putting together crews for future missions to Mars.

1   **A** uncertain   **B** unfitting   **C** unbelievable   **D** unlikely

2   **A** representing   **B** pretending   **C** simulating   **D** imitating

3   **A** reason   **B** object   **C** ideal   **D** ambition

4   **A** achieve   **B** store   **C** gather   **D** deduce

5   **A** views   **B** points   **C** aspects   **D** qualities

6   **A** delights   **B** fortunes   **C** merits   **D** luxuries

7   **A** conduct   **B** operate   **C** practise   **D** follow

8   **A** relevance   **B** connection   **C** influence   **D** application

Part 2

For questions **9–16**, read the text below and think of the word which best fits each gap. Use only **one** word in each gap. There is an example at the beginning (**0**).
Write your answers **IN CAPITAL LETTERS on the separate answer sheet**.

Example: | **0** | | *O* | *R* | | | | | | | | | | | | | | | | | |

Human body rhythms

I'm a scientist and I study human body rhythms, **(0)** …….. circadian rhythms as they are called. Everything in our body is rhythmic; we used to think that there was just one 'clock' in the brain controlling these rhythms, **(9)** …….. we now know that we have clocks in just about **(10)** …….. tissue in our body. We are trying to understand how they interact with one another and the way they are affected by time cues **(11)** …….. light or meal times. Scientists study these rhythms **(12)** …….. we can help people, for example, to synchronise to new time zones and also help those **(13)** …….. circadian rhythms are out of balance.

What currently interests me is the link between the timing of our body clocks and our metabolism. We know, for example, that long-term shift workers seem to desire sugary things such as biscuits and this can lead **(14)** …….. health problems. Why **(15)** …….. is the case requires a lot more research. My colleagues and I are working **(16)** …….. finding a link at the moment.

Part 3

For questions **17–24**, read the text below. Use the word given in capitals at the end of some of the lines to form a word that fits in the gap **in the same line**. There is an example at the beginning (**0**). Write your answers **IN CAPITAL LETTERS on the separate answer sheet**.

Example:

0	M	I	L	L	I	O	N	A	I	R	E							

The young entrepreneur

It's probably fair to say that self-made (**0**) …….. undergraduates are   **MILLION**

something of a (**17**) …….. . But then, even by Oxford University's   **RARE**

standards, Nick D'Aloisio is a rather (**18**) …….. student.   **ORDINARY**

Always (**19**) …….. inquisitive, D'Aloisio taught himself programming   **INTELLECT**

while relatively young. He used his new-found expertise to create

a mobile phone app which summarises news articles. He called it

Summly. But D'Aloisio is also highly (**20**) …….. and, aged only 15, he   **AMBITION**

sought and then received financial backing from several (**21**) …….. ,   **INVEST**

which allowed him to develop his technology. It proved (**22**) ……..   **PHENOMENON**

successful and two years later the multinational corporation, Yahoo,

acquired D'Aloisio's app for $30 million. He then worked for the US

tech giant for a time (there was some (**23**) …….. in his team about   **SCEPTIC**

having a 17-year-old product manager!) before deciding to continue

his studies.

Despite his huge wealth, D'Aloisio thinks that equating money with

success is never a good idea and feels (**24**) …….. to be treated just   **FORTUNE**

like any other student by both teachers and peers.

Part 4

For questions **25–30**, complete the second sentence so that it has a similar meaning to the first sentence, using the word given. **Do not change the word given**. You must use between **three** and **six** words, including the word given. Here is an example (**0**).

Example:

0   James would only speak to the head of department alone.

   ON

   James ………………………………………………… to the head of department alone.

The gap can be filled by the words 'insisted on speaking', so you write:

Example:

0	*INSISTED ON SPEAKING*

Write **only** the missing words **IN CAPITAL LETTERS on the separate answer sheet**.

---

25   Carol's plan was to finish her paintings by spring.

   SUPPOSED

   Carol's paintings …………………………………... by spring.

26   All the runners received a medal when they completed the marathon.

   COMPLETION

   Every …………………………………... of the marathon.

27   What are your plans for the company's tenth anniversary celebrations?

   MIND

   What do …………………………………... the company's tenth anniversary celebrations?

28 You might not get the job, but you've got nothing to lose by applying.

HARM

You might not get the job, but ………………………………….. applying.

29 In Marco's opinion, there was no reason to buy a car.

CONCERNED

As …………………………………... , there was no reason to buy a car.

30 The manager was unsure whether to employ someone with so little experience.

RESERVATIONS

The manager …………………………………... someone with so little experience.

Part 5

You are going to read an article about anthropomorphism – attributing human characteristics or behaviour to animals. For questions **31–36**, choose the answer (**A**, **B**, **C** or **D**) which you think fits best according to the text. Mark your answers **on the separate answer sheet**.

Are humans and animals really so different?

Science correspondent Martha Hamlin looks at whether anthropomorphism – attributing human characteristics or behavior to animals – is necessarily a bad thing

One night not long ago, an octopus named Inky hauled himself out of his tank at New Zealand's National Aquarium, heaved himself across the floor and squeezed into a narrow drain leading to the Pacific Ocean. It was a story fit for a children's film, and was widely shared online. Part of the fun of the story and other such tales of escape, involving creatures as diverse as rats and llamas, is indulging in a bit of knowing anthropomorphism: animals, they're just like us! In the case of octopuses, this pleasure is especially pronounced, because the creatures' great intelligence comes packaged in bodies so vastly dissimilar to our own. How is it that eight-tentacled sea creatures can open jars, recognize faces, use coconut shells as portable armor and even exhibit sophisticated play behavior?

Anthropomorphism is often thought of as unscientific, but Dr. Frans de Waal, who studies primates such as gorillas and chimpanzees, argues that it is not in fact anthropomorphizing, but its opposite – an unwillingness to recognize the human-like traits of animals, or what he terms anthropodenial – that has too often characterized our attitudes toward other species. Analysing decades of animal-cognition research, he shows that, with the exception of fully-developed language, animals have been observed exhibiting many of the key behaviors that were thought to distinguish humans from animals: the ability to consider the past and the future, to demonstrate empathy and self-awareness, and to anticipate the motives of others. Animals, in other words, are far smarter than we've been giving them credit for.

Anthropodenial, in de Waal's opinion, is a relatively modern phenomenon. In medieval and early modern Europe, the animal mind was considered sophisticated enough that animals could be put on trial for crimes. And as recently as the nineteenth century, many naturalists sought out the connections between human and animal intelligence. 'The difference in mind between man and the higher animals, great as it is, certainly is one of degree and not of kind,' one nineteenth-century naturalist wrote. And this was no radical supporter of animal rights; it was Charles Darwin, whose theory of evolution changed the way we understand our place in the world.

The advent of behaviorism in the twentieth century, with its emphasis on conditioning animals through reward and punishment, shifted public views of animal intelligence. For most of the twentieth century, the two dominant schools of thought viewed animals as either stimulus-response machines or as robots endowed with useful instincts. It is perhaps no accident that this shift occurred during the same century that saw humans tearing down animal habitats at unprecedented rates, polluting land and water, and developing methods of rearing livestock which ignored the welfare of the animals.

Happily, de Waal believes that we are emerging from this dark period and learning to think of animal cognition as being on the same spectrum, though not necessarily at the same point, as that of humans. *line 63* 'The times are changing,' he writes. 'Everyone must have noticed the avalanche of knowledge emerging over the last few decades, diffused over the internet.' The most effective tests of animal intelligence, he argues, are designed with a species' particular traits and skills in mind. Squirrels may fail at human memory tasks, but whereas we need apps to find our misplaced phones, they can remember where they've hidden tiny caches of nuts. In her book *The Soul of an Octopus*, naturalist Sy Montgomery points out that if an octopus were to measure human intelligence, it might test us on the number of color patterns we can produce on our skin. Seeing us fail the test, it might conclude that we are pretty stupid.

De Waal remains skeptical of Inky's happy ending. He points out that, while captive octopuses have escaped their tanks before, it's probably overly optimistic to think that Inky figured out how to get to a drain leading to the ocean. But de Waal is aware of the power of viral stories to fuel appreciation of animal intelligence. He once ran an experiment to test whether capuchin monkeys can experience envy. When the monkeys were rewarded with either cucumbers (a well-liked monkey food) or grapes (an even better one), those given cucumbers shrieked and raged at seeing their peers get the superior treat. The study was published in a prominent scientific journal soon afterwards. But what really convinced people of the findings was a one-minute video clip of the experiment, released ten years later. Just one of the oddities of our particular kind of animal mind.

31   What point does the writer make about octopuses in the first paragraph?

    A   Their playful nature would make them a good subject for a children's film.
    B   They are no more likely to be able to escape captivity than any other creature.
    C   People still underestimate their intelligence despite what is known about their abilities.
    D   Their human-like behaviour surprises people more as they are so unlike humans in appearance.

32   In the second paragraph, the writer says that Dr. Frans de Waal

    A   gave a more accurate name to a changing behaviour.
    B   conducted experiments to back up his arguments.
    C   came to a conclusion based on existing data.
    D   questioned the research of other scientists.

33   In the third paragraph, the writer emphasises the fact that

    A   accepting de Waal's ideas requires people to alter the way they see themselves.
    B   human knowledge has progressed considerably since medieval times.
    C   putting animals on trial was not universally considered reasonable.
    D   de Waal's views are backed up by the work of respected scientists.

34   What does 'that' in line 63 refer to?

    A   dark period
    B   cognition
    C   spectrum
    D   point

35   What is the main idea put forward in the fifth paragraph?

    A   Even with technology, humans are unable to match animal abilities.
    B   Being able to test other species doesn't mean you are superior to them.
    C   It is logical to assess a species' intelligence according to its unique abilities.
    D   The internet has played a major role in changing people's views of animal intelligence.

36   In the last paragraph, the writer thinks it is significant that

    A   a video has more impact on people than written data.
    B   people are interested in whether monkeys can feel envy.
    C   de Waal waited ten years to release the video of his experiment.
    D   people invent a happy ending if a story doesn't already have one.

Part 6

You are going to read four extracts from articles in which architects discuss their profession. For questions **37–40**, choose from the architects **A–D**. The architects may be chosen more than once. Mark your answers **on the separate answer sheet**.

The nature of architecture

Four architects talk about their profession

A What I love about architecture is that it's the only one of the applied arts that can change how we perceive the world around us. But however much I love buildings, even I recognise that, as much as we may want to, we will not be able to save them all. Buildings are constantly being degraded, attacked by the elements as well as by simple use. In any case, there are plenty of buildings that we wouldn't want to hold on to. Building design is a complex thing, and a space which ultimately doesn't work has never been created that way deliberately. It's just that it's impossible to predict everything before a building is complete. Going forward, there has to be a recognition of what is good for the planet in terms of building design. Our needs are changing rapidly, particularly regarding energy use, and energy efficiency will be a major theme in architecture.

B Modern life places demands on buildings which are different from those of the past, meaning that not all heritage buildings can or should be kept. Decisions must be made as to which are of most benefit to a community. It's the same with the design of new buildings. Their primary function is to improve the lives of the occupants. What good are stunning aesthetics if someone inside is stifled by heat from a badly placed window? As to creativity, an architect has to design according to the client's brief, so self-expression, such a key factor in the world of art, plays little part. Opinions on the new building will inevitably differ, and thanks to modern technology, these can be shared far more widely and quickly than in the past – often even as a building is under construction. This immediacy of feedback is sure to play a big part in building design over the coming decades.

C Architecture as a profession grew from the human need for shelter, but buildings have become a form of identity for the culture in which they're located, and their design must revolve around this idea. A well-designed building is a work of art which improves the appearance of the area in which it is placed. In addition, we can, and must, learn from it. How can we create a vibrant environment consisting of exciting and remarkable built forms if we allow the great achievements of the past to crumble away? Even the buildings which might be considered 'bad' still have something to offer. They are a reminder that perfect architecture doesn't exist. Architects don't have the luxury of creating a prototype, unlike, for example, a car designer, so unforeseen mistakes will creep in from time to time.

D When I look at those buildings which are almost universally criticised, or which clearly don't work for their users, I see the hand of an arrogant architect who believes that their right to self-expression should be given priority over aspects such as local context. I'm not denying for a moment that architecture is an art form, but the primary consideration must always be the user of the building. As architects, we have both the opportunity and the responsibility to create designs in which the experience of the building's inhabitants and others who interact with it will be enriched. While I don't see that changing, other things will come into play over the next few years. As the world's population rises, space and resources are becoming more limited, so inevitably, concerns over increasing global temperatures and greenhouse gas emissions will be reflected more in the buildings we create.

Which architect

has a similar opinion to D regarding future influences on architecture? | 37 | |

shares an opinion with A on whether architecture should be preserved? | 38 | |

expresses a different view from the other three on whether architecture is art? | 39 | |

has a different opinion to B on the most important factor to consider when designing a building? | 40 | |

Part 7

You are going to read an extract from a website article about the collections belonging to natural history museums. Six paragraphs have been removed from the article. Choose from the paragraphs **A–G** the one which fits each gap (**41–46**). There is one extra paragraph which you do not need to use. Mark your answers **on the separate answer sheet**.

Natural history museums are teeming with undiscovered species

Tracking them down is a globe-trotting adventure that rivals any jungle expedition

I recently visited the American Museum of Natural History (AMNH) in New York, in the company of Evon Hekkala, a geneticist at the nearby Fordham University. She is a vocal advocate for natural history museums and the many secrets that remain locked within their drawers and displays.

41	

But to Hekkala and many other scientists, they are full of riches. They are time capsules that contain records of past ecosystems that are rapidly changing or disappearing. They are archives that provide clues about raging epidemics, environmental pollution, and hidden extinctions. And they are full of unknown species.

42	

She found 16 in the AMNH alone, collected almost a century ago, and dozens more from other institutions. From each specimen, she picked off fragments of dried tissue, still rich in viable DNA. She even managed to sequence DNA from seven mummified specimens from a museum in Paris. The mummies are around two thousand years old, but thanks to the Egyptians' skill at preservation, Hekkala found enough to use.

43	

In the AMNH, Hekkala pulls out several drawers containing examples of both to show me. The adjacent shelves are full of other reptilian remains. 'One of my students used these collections to show that there are three species within what we thought of as the Nile monitor lizard,' she says.

'Another student is working on hinged tortoises. I predict that we probably have 100 unrecognized species in these collections, just sitting on the shelves.'

44	

None of this would be possible without advances in modern technology, and in fact every development opens up fresh ways of exploiting these old treasures. Using next-generation sequencing techniques, scientists can extract DNA from the unlikeliest of sources, even animals that have been submerged in embalming liquid. They can pull out isotopes of carbon and nitrogen that reveal what an animal was eating and they can identify pollutants.

45	

And by discovering entirely new species in this way, as with the Western sacred crocodile, it is possible to create plans to protect them. 'There's been tons of oil exploration in the sacred crocodile's range in West Africa,' says Hekkala. 'But now we know it's there, we can try to get protections put in place. We can still hold on to it if we know it's there.'

46	

That's because the act of collecting sacrifices a few individual lives, but in return, it gives us irreplaceable information about hidden species and about how our wildlife is reacting to our changing world. The dramatic dwindling of the planet's diversity – the so-called sixth extinction – makes such work more critical, not less.

A That's why the act of collecting still matters. A recent opinion piece, published in the journal *Science*, argued that specimen-collecting risked killing off vulnerable species, and should be supplanted by audio recordings, camera-trap images, and non-lethal tissue gathering. It drew a loud response from more than 100 biologists, who argued that none of those strategies beats having an actual specimen.

B Together, the samples corroborated Hekkala's suspicions: the Nile crocodile was indeed two separate species. The Eastern one has two fewer chromosomes than the Western sacred crocodile. It seems that at one time they co-existed along the full length of the Nile, but today they stick to different parts of Africa. They only share space in museums.

C Capturing this information about the environment involves a huge amount of work so Hekkala is trying to create an army of young scientists who are willing to help her with it. 'It's great that people are still keen on going on expeditions,' she says. 'But to be honest we can achieve the same thing by simply looking in the drawers of museums.'

D It's easy to view the collections kept in such places as soulless stashes, examples of humanity's hoarding instinct unleashed upon the natural world, turning vibrant wildlife into mere specimens, disassembled and dissected, pinned onto boards, crammed into cabinets, and stuffed into jars.

E Many unclassified species on the other hand are still taking up valuable space and gathering dust in jars. The legendary naturalists of yesteryear catalogued life's grand diversity by hopping across continents and islands, but their modern counterparts don't need to put in this much effort.

F Hekkala stumbled across one of these herself while sequencing DNA from Nile crocodile samples collected all over Africa, in a bid to understand differences between the various populations of this reptile. 'Because I'm a museum geek, I thought: Oh, I can get tons of Nile croc specimens from museum collections,' she says.

G However, the specimens reveal more to science than the mere identities of their owners. Their sizes and shapes show how bodies adapt: how songbirds become smaller as the climate gets hotter. Their DNA reveals how some endangered species have experienced plummeting levels of diversity, while others have started to regain their lost genetic wealth.

Part 8

You are going to read an article about the sources which university students can use for their essays. For questions **47–56**, choose from the sections (**A–D**). The sections may be chosen more than once. Mark your answers **on the separate answer sheet**.

In which section does the writer

ask about the specific details regarding a rule change?	47
bring the existence of a particular group into question?	48
mention a factor which has made a distinction less clear?	49
argue that it is useful to learn how to assess whether or not a source is valid?	50
mention weaknesses in an extract which can be exploited?	51
state that a particular custom leads to division and prejudice?	52
say that a change could increase students' confidence?	53
mention writers whose work is read by both academics and the public?	54
explore the choices available in a particular dilemma?	55
insist that she is not in favour of abandoning the current system?	56

Scholarly sources versus popular sources

'There is an abundance of serious material outside academia, so why not use it?'
asks university professor Rachel Harvey

A A student is researching scholarly material for her essay. She finds a quote she thinks she can use. It ticks all the boxes: original and insightful, persuasively argued, provocative, and with just enough holes that a good forensic analysis will have something to expose. There's one problem, however. It does not come from an academic paper, but from a blog written by an obscure amateur. It has, technically speaking, no academic credibility. By convention, students – and academics – are supposed only to engage in critical discussion with 'academically credible' sources. What, then, is the student to do? Pretend this precious nugget doesn't exist? A terrible waste. Plagiarise it (after all, who'll know)? Completely unethical. I'm not talking here about the sourcing of facts, or the fraught issue of truth and objectivity. I'm focusing on ideas, opinions and theories and my central argument is that we do our research a disservice if we automatically exclude a source because its provenance does not match certain outmoded criteria.

B The line between 'credible' and 'non-credible' sources is becoming ever more blurred, particularly in the era of electronic self-publishing. The internet has undoubtedly democratised the spread of ideas, weakening the assumption that university departments have some kind of monopoly on cogent, logical thinking. But if the line on permissible sources were to be moved, where should it be redrawn? If an official university department blog were deemed acceptable for students to cite, for instance, what about the personal blog of a leading professor or research student? What about publications by accredited and respected museums and galleries? And what of those whose published books and articles straddle the border between academia and general readership? Would their more popular works be considered less suitable for essay purposes than the less accessible ones? To take art theory as another example, where do we stand on those critics who write for a general readership? Is it acceptable to engage in argument only with well-established names?

C There are no easy answers, and I wouldn't dream of suggesting that we completely cast aside the challenging and rigorous in favour of the populist and amateur. Yet the assertion that only papers and books published by universities and their partners and associates are worthy of students' critical engagement does seem to foster a kind of academic protectionism which can't easily be justified. The convention of referring to academic writers exclusively by their surname and the publication date of their text is part of the problem. The effect is to create a kind of 'them and us' attitude, the idea of the grand academic being such a renowned authority on the topic that we don't even introduce them by their full name: they simply don't need one. So you've never heard of Jones (2003)? That's because you're just not on his/her intellectual plane. The surname-only principle implies that flimsiest of notions, the 'academic community', a kind of exclusive club for those who jealously guard rigorous debate and the exchange of ideas. Arguably, this 'club' has never been a real community in any meaningful sense.

D Far better to introduce academic writers by their full names, with a brief description of who they are, as we already do with sources from outside the so-called academic community. So Jones (2003) would be introduced as Pat Jones, senior lecturer in media studies at X University, in much the same way as we introduce, say, fashion blogger Tim Smith, jewellery designer Lena Thomas or film reviewer Mick Stuart. That way students could be actively encouraged to collate ideas and arguments from multitudinous sources from both inside and outside academia – and ultimately to decide for themselves which ones deserve closer scrutiny on the basis of intrinsic merit. It might even encourage them to become less timid about criticising theory in their own words, based on their own insights. Some will say this would lead to a horrendous free-for-all, where no distinction is made between learned discourse and undisciplined chattering. But sorting the valuable from the worthless and identifying bias, prejudice and sheer self-indulgence is always an intellectually exhilarating task that sharpens one's critical skills – wherever the debate is taking place.

WRITING (1 hour 30 minutes)

Part 1

You **must** answer this question. Write your answer in **220–260** words in an appropriate style **on the separate answer sheet**.

1   Your class has just watched a video about ways of protecting endangered species. You have made the notes below:

Ways of protecting endangered species:

*   raising awareness among young people
*   restoring natural habitats
*   captive breeding programmes

Some opinions expressed in the discussion:

"Many children have little or no contact with animals these days."

"We need a global commitment to keeping the habitats animals need."

"Keeping some endangered animals in captivity may help them to breed successfully."

Write an essay for your tutor discussing **two** of the ways in your notes. You should **explain which way of protecting endangered species you think is likely to be more effective, giving reasons** in support of your opinion.

You may, if you wish, make use of the opinions expressed in the discussion, but you should use your own words as far as possible.

Part 2

Write an answer to **one** of the questions **2–4** in this part. Write your answer in **220–260** words in an appropriate style **on the separate answer sheet**. Put the question number in the box at the top of the page.

---

2   You have recently completed the first year at college. You think it would be useful if there was an introductory session for new students. You decide to send a proposal for such a session to the Principal. In your proposal, you should explain why you think an introductory session would be useful for new students, summarise your ideas for its content and suggest how current students could be involved.

Write your **proposal**.

3   You have recently taken a course to improve a practical skill – for example, IT or cookery. The course director has asked you to write a report on the course.

In your report, you should explain which parts of the course proved successful, comment on aspects you felt did not work so well and suggest how the course could be improved.

Write your **report**.

4   A piece of land in the centre of the town where you live is available for development. The editor of a local newspaper has asked residents to comment on the suggestions which have been made by the town council to build either a shopping mall or a sports centre.

You decide to write a letter to the editor evaluating the two options, explaining which would be better for the local community and why.

Write your **letter**. You do not need to include postal addresses.

LISTENING (approximately 40 minutes)

Part 1

You will hear three different extracts. For questions **1–6**, choose the answer (**A**, **B** or **C**) which fits best according to what you hear. There are two questions for each extract.

Listening test audio

Extract One

You hear a man telling a friend about his recent visit to his parents at the home where he grew up.

1 How did he feel while he was there?

    A keen to re-establish ties with his siblings

    B surprised by his reactions to seemingly trivial things

    C happy about refreshing his memories of familiar surroundings

2 The woman responds to the man's story by

    A dismissing what he has said as pure exaggeration.

    B contributing examples of her own family experiences.

    C recognising that he has touched on something fundamental.

Extract Two

You hear two people discussing 3D printing in relation to wildlife and nature conservation.

3 The man believes that treating an injured bird using 3D printing

    A is hard to justify financially.

    B was simply a publicity stunt.

    C has highlighted local problems.

4 They both think that 3D printing techniques

    A aren't fast enough to aid coral reef restoration.

    B will soon be producing artificial coral worldwide.

    C might be able to help restore damaged coral reefs.

Extract Three

You hear two high school students discussing playing musical instruments.

5   The girl thinks that playing a musical instrument

    A is an effective way to socialise.

    B can impact positively on physical pursuits.

    C might improve academic progress.

6   What does the boy intend to do following the conversation?

    A reassess his approach to learning

    B do some research on the benefits of music

    C intensify his efforts to achieve an ambition

Part 2

You will hear a man called Pat Coolidge talking about his career as an information technology entrepreneur.
For questions **7–14**, complete the sentences with a word or short phrase.

Listening test audio

IT entrepreneur

Pat first became interested in working with information technology while in Paris studying

(7) ....

On moving to California, Pat found work as a so-called **(8)** ....

responsible for acquiring new customers.

While he was in California, Pat decided a course on **(9)** .... would

benefit him in his entrepreneurial activities.

In order to see more of the world, Pat decided to offer his services as a

(10) ....

When describing himself and his particular way of life, Pat calls himself a

(11) ....

Pat and his friends were reluctant to found a new company because of potential financial

problems finding the **(12)** .... necessary.

The top priority at Pat's new venture, *Manatee*, is to foster the

(13) .... of those involved.

Pat favours the word **(14)** .... to describe each branch of *Manatee*.

Part 3

You will hear part of a podcast of a college lecturer interviewing two Film Studies students, Samuel and Anna, about a work placement they have just completed. For questions **15–20**, choose the answer (**A**, **B**, **C** or **D**) which fits best according to what you hear.

Listening test audio

---

15 Samuel and Anna chose to apply to Blandford Films for a placement because
   A the company website included plenty of information on hosting students.
   B a college teacher had once done some work for the company.
   C the company was recommended by a previous graduate.
   D they read a description of the company in a film journal.

16 What does Anna think persuaded the company to accept her and Samuel on the placement?
   A their ideas for future film projects
   B their mature analysis of the film industry
   C their extensive experience of film making
   D their openness to new film making approaches

17 What impression did Samuel have of the company during the first week of the placement?
   A It required high levels of commitment from its employees.
   B It was an intimidating environment for a new person.
   C It was difficult to find out what tasks he was being assigned.
   D It would take a while to understand how the company operates.

18 When they started the placement, Anna was surprised about
   A the size of the company premises.
   B the number of projects being run at one time.
   C the main source of income for the company.
   D the approach staff had to adopt to their work.

19 What does Samuel think was the most valuable thing he learned from doing the placement?
   A that people respect you for defending your views
   B the importance of attention to detail in the film industry
   C what it takes to manage large numbers of creative people
   D that it's unwise to question more experienced colleagues

20 Anna and Samuel both advise students applying for any work placement to
   A find out about the length of the working day.
   B be honest about any gaps in knowledge and skills.
   C have a proper holiday before doing the placement.
   D be prepared to travel to find the best placement.

Part 4

You will hear five short extracts in which people are talking about their experiences of living in tall buildings.

Listening test audio

TASK ONE

For questions **21–25**, choose from the list **(A–H)** why each speaker decided to live in the building.

TASK TWO

For questions **26–30**, choose from the list **(A–H)** what surprised each speaker about living in the building.

While you listen, you must complete both tasks.

A	its affordability		A	the feeling of social isolation	
B	the novelty of the experience		B	the contrast with previous experiences	
C	its proximity to family		C	the helpfulness of neighbours	
D	its convenient location		D	the expansive view	
E	a personal recommendation		E	the number of repairs needed	
F	a retreat from city noise		F	the opportunity to relax	
G	its prestigious address		G	the efficient maintenance services	
H	its conventional appearance		H	the sense of security	

Speaker 1		21	Speaker 1	26
Speaker 2		22	Speaker 2	27
Speaker 3		23	Speaker 3	28
Speaker 4		24	Speaker 4	29
Speaker 5		25	Speaker 5	30

Test 2

Icon	What does it mean?
🔊	Listening test audio (Scan the QR code or download from the Resource Bank)

Test 2

READING AND USE OF ENGLISH (1 hour 30 minutes)

Part 1

For questions **1–8**, read the text below and decide which answer (**A**, **B**, **C** or **D**) best fits each gap. There is an example at the beginning (**0**).
Mark your answers **on the separate answer sheet**.

Example:

0 **A** reviewing   **B** considering   **C** observing   **D** inspecting

| **0** | A
o | B
● | C
o | D
o |

How do frogs jump such long distances?

When **(0)** .... whether it is muscle strength that produces the powerful movements of certain animals, it is important to remember frogs. A mistaken **(1)** .... many of us make is that animals which produce powerful movements attain this power through having large muscles. But the abilities of frogs **(2)** .... to the fact that this is not always the **(3)** .... They lack huge muscles, yet are capable of leaping very long distances.

Researchers Thomas Roberts and Henry Astley have shown that, in fact, the secret of frogs' abilities **(4)** .... in elastic mechanisms in their legs. They used 3D X-ray video and scanning technology to keep **(5)** .... of changes in a frog's legs before, during and after a leap. The images supply **(6)** .... of how the leg tendons act like springs, releasing stored-up energy to propel the frog forward. This is what accounts for the truly exceptional jumping abilities of frogs.

According to Roberts, while frogs are interesting in their own **(7)** .... , their study also provides **(8)** .... into how elastic mechanisms in tendons may work in animal movement generally.

1 **A** outlook   **B** reasoning   **C** assumption   **D** logic

2 **A** point   **B** indicate   **C** refer   **D** illustrate

3 **A** condition   **B** matter   **C** case   **D** model

4 **A** holds   **B** lies   **C** stems   **D** stays

5 **A** pace   **B** touch   **C** place   **D** track

6 **A** data   **B** material   **C** evidence   **D** backing

7 **A** right   **B** concern   **C** style   **D** aspect

8 **A** understanding   **B** vision   **C** perception   **D** insight

Part 2

For questions **9–16**, read the text below and think of the word which best fits each gap. Use only **one** word in each gap. There is an example at the beginning (**0**).
Write your answers **IN CAPITAL LETTERS on the separate answer sheet**.

Example:

0		I	N															

Stepping into the boss's shoes

Your manager is away and you've been asked to stand (**0**) .... for them. Regardless of (**9**) .... it's only for a few days or a whole month, such responsibility is simultaneously exciting and terrifying. Most of us, (**10**) .... we're honest, want our boss's job, so (**11**) .... on the role temporarily is an opportunity worth seizing. In the future, you might want to apply for their job, so (**12**) .... the most of any chance to prove you have what it takes.

Is your boss (**13**) .... of those people who checks emails on holiday and never quite turns off? Then it's probably tempting to contact them about your decisions. This is bad for just about (**14**) .... concerned: your boss won't have a restful break and you, (**15**) .... you may not realise it, are unconsciously proving you're not ready for more responsibility. So be brave. There's no need to make drastic changes, just take a deep breath and go (**16**) .... your instincts.

Part 3

For questions **17–24**, read the text below. Use the word given in capitals at the end of some of the lines to form a word that fits in the gap **in the same line**. There is an example at the beginning (**0**). Write your answers **IN CAPITAL LETTERS on the separate answer sheet**.

Example: | 0 | D | R | A | M | A | T | I | C | A | L | L | Y | | | | | | | |

Unstaffed shops in Sweden

Over recent decades, the number of small shops in rural Sweden has been falling **(0)** .... For reasons related to the economy and a declining population, these shop **(17)** .... have affected numerous isolated villages.

DRAMA
CLOSE

However, with the opening of unstaffed supermarkets, now the way people shop has **(18)** .... a radical change. To enter, all that is needed is a code from the shop's app. Once inside there are no assistants, and shoppers make their selections from a range of basic daily **(19)** .... , for example, milk or bread. The shop's app is also used to process any **(20)** .... which need to be made.

GO

NECESSARY
PAY

At first shoppers admitted to feeling slightly **(21)** .... at having no one to say 'Hi' to, but they soon became accustomed to the new system. Previously, buying food had involved a drive to the nearest town, but the unstaffed shop has **(22)** .... local people to stock up without this **(23)** ....

COMFORT

ABLE
CONVENIENT

Indeed, the idea has proved so popular that the company behind the scheme plans an **(24)** .... of the network in the near future.

EXPAND

Part 4

For questions **25–30**, complete the second sentence so that it has a similar meaning to the first sentence, using the word given. **Do not change the word given.** You must use between **three** and **six** words, including the word given. Here is an example (**0**).

Example:

0   James would only speak to the head of department alone.

ON

James ………………………………………………… to the head of department alone.

The gap can be filled with the words 'insisted on speaking', so you write:

Example:	**0**	*INSISTED ON SPEAKING*

Write **only** the missing words **IN CAPITAL LETTERS on the separate answer sheet**.

---

25   Tim thinks Peter's work is poor.

OPINION

Tim doesn't …………………………………... Peter's work.

26   Compared to her previous essay, it's clear that Emma tried a lot harder with this one.

EFFORT

It's clear that Emma put much …………………………………... her previous one.

27   Sarah usually gives bad news by email, rather than talking to staff face-to-face.

AVOID

Sarah tends …………………………………... person, and sends an email to staff instead.

28 'Simon, you must stop getting angry during classes,' said his teacher.

TEMPER

Simon was warned by his teacher to ………………………….…... control during classes.

29 'I'm happy to listen to suggestions,' Penny told her staff.

OPEN

Penny let her staff ……………………………….... suggestions.

30 The other five-star hotels in the city centre are considerably less expensive than the Grand.

MOST

The Grand is by ……………………………….... all the five-star hotels in the city centre.

Part 5

You are going to read an article about Skip Lievsay, a sound editor and mixer. For questions **31–36**, choose the answer (**A**, **B**, **C** or **D**) which you think fits best according to the text.
Mark your answers **on the separate answer sheet**.

Skip Lievsay – the sound master

Lievsay is a supervising sound editor and mixer for film and television

When I went to interview Skip Lievsay, I found an ordinary-looking man standing before the stacks of speakers and the giant movie screen in his office. You might imagine that a preeminent sound engineer in the film industry would have a dominating presence, but Lievsay doesn't fit that mold. Whatever he does – whether it's operating the sound console or giving instructions to the employees in his New York offices – his demeanor is calm and his voice low. Underlying Lievsay's manner is his belief, firmly held, that his work is about patience and craftsmanship, not novelty and sudden flashes of creativity. That's why he and the team he supervises spend days trying to get the right effect for a few seconds of film.

Most film-goers take the audioscape of a movie for granted, and assume visual continuity is trickier to achieve. But after a movie goes through picture editing, it's handed off to the sound supervisor, who oversees the various elements of sound design, editing and mixing. The distinction between these three processes is subtle: design and editing have more to do with the development and selection of the sounds that make up each scene. Mixing involves taking these sounds and integrating them into each scene so everything sounds 'natural' – in other words, ensuring the sound of a butterfly landing on a car hood isn't louder than the car backfiring.

It is a central principle of sound editing that people hear what they are conditioned to hear, not what they're actually hearing. The sound of rain in movies? Frying eggs. Car engines revving in a chase scene? It's partly engines, but what gives it that visceral, gut-level grist is lions' roars mixed in. To be excellent, a sound editor needs not just a perceptive, trained ear, but also a gift for imagining what a sound *could* do, what someone else *might* hear.

Despite Lievsay's contribution to multiple hit films, you've probably never heard of him.

He and his team are only a few among the legions involved in film production who go about their painstaking, essential work far from the limelight. But while he might not be a household name, he's famous among people who are in the public eye. Whereas some sound engineers might go for a layered effect, Lievsay is all about finding the one, precise sound that tells us everything we need to know. He understands that sound helps us orient ourselves in relation to space and to each other, and that our ears know, precognitively, when a dark room has someone lurking in it.

I observed Lievsay as he was reviewing a scene of a man dropping in on his wife's dance rehearsal. The director had wanted a 'matter-of-fact' sound to suggest the couple were carving a special moment out of something not special, but the scene felt 'dreamy'. Lievsay fiddled with a few dials for a moment, and then replayed the scene. It was then that I realized something fundamental about film-making, and about sound editing in particular. I'd watched it before but now something extraordinary happened. I noticed a receptionist passing behind the wife. Lievsay had given her footsteps. Without the footsteps, I'd somehow never seen her; now, I saw her, and her presence – along with a few other Lievsay tweaks – suggested people at work, things happening outside the eye contact between husband and wife. I saw the entire scene differently.

There is something unnerving about spending time around individuals whose powers of perception suggest the existence of another layer of reality you are missing. The way Lievsay and his colleagues work requires a completely different – almost unnatural – way of experiencing sound. 'Our process reflects that each sound is important enough to deserve its own consideration,' Lievsay says.

31 What does the writer suggest about Skip Lievsay in the first paragraph?

    A He expects others to be equally committed to the job.
    B He seems unassuming for a person in his line of work.
    C He is modest about the importance of his artistic output.
    D He is reluctant to project an authoritarian image.

32 What is the writer doing in the second paragraph?

    A explaining which aspect of film making is most controversial
    B speculating on why a particular belief has become widespread
    C pointing out the kind of errors which affect a film's credibility
    D drawing attention to how complex a sound supervisor's work is

33 The writer mentions rain and car engines in order to

    A show how certain sounds can be replicated.
    B suggest which sounds stimulate certain emotions.
    C provide examples of sounds that are common in films.
    D illustrate some of the hardest challenges for sound engineers.

34 When talking about Lievsay's contribution to film, the writer

    A is frustrated by the fact that so few people know who he is.
    B doubts that his contemporaries share his range of skills.
    C appreciates his determination to find the perfect sound.
    D implies that he makes best use of sound in dramatic scenes.

35 What point is the writer making when he talks about the dance rehearsal scene?

    A Even the most experienced sound editors have to follow instructions.
    B A small aural cue can affect our understanding of narrative.
    C Sound and vision have an equal role to play in holding our attention.
    D The wrong sound will cause distraction in a scene rather than enhance it.

36 From the text as a whole, we understand that the writer

    A respects Lievsay for his professionalism.
    B is anxious to defend Lievsay from his critics.
    C intends to emulate Lievsay as a sound editor.
    D suspects that Lievsay may be hard to impress.

Part 6

You are going to read four extracts from articles in which experts give their views on rewilding, the practice of reintroducing animals and plants into their original habitats. For questions **37–40**, choose from the experts **A–D**. The experts may be chosen more than once.
Mark your answers **on the separate answer sheet**.

Rewilding

A That rewilding can marry economic and ecological priorities is a message which campaigners are beginning to communicate to national governments. Policy makers see that altering land-use patterns away from farming can enable the development of, for example, new areas for walkers, and can lead to new revenue generated from the leisure facilities catering for them. The other side of this win-win coin is that the carbon captured in letting nature regenerate will be crucial if we are to stop the atmosphere heating up any further. That said, while government ministers are starting to see the light, the same can't be said for the public, especially with other aspects of rewilding, such as species reintroduction. The media often carries enthusiastic stories about unofficial releases of animals into areas to which they aren't actually adapted. This risks the creation of something like artificial safari parks. However, now isn't the time to decelerate, and the roll-out of wider schemes must be prioritised.

B Considering the amount of recent media attention rewilding has received, it should come as no surprise that many people are extremely literate on the subject. The number and diversity of projects reported daily is mind-boggling and reflects, in my opinion, the fact that the brakes need to be applied. However, the benefits in terms of absorbing greenhouse gases by, for instance, converting agriculturally unproductive highlands back to their natural forested state are so great that perhaps the pace of change will actually increase. Economists will push forcefully, citing potential profits, but it is this approach that led to the original environmental degradation – financial gain shouldn't enter into the equation when there's the prospect of re-establishing natural forests and stocking them with their original rightful inhabitants.

C Although TV schedules have been saturated with wildlife programmes for decades, when asked, most people seem to equate rewilding with the reintroduction of 'signature species', typically large mammals like beavers. To appreciate that it is a wider phenomenon concerning habitat renewal, a concerted information campaign is required. Only then will the full benefits be understood; we will see animals back in their natural surroundings, as well as enhanced incomes for farmers from diversified land use. That said, it can be a double-edged sword. Reassigning land away from practices which generate gases and cause climate change must be set against the need to compensate for any subsequent domestic food supply shortfall. This might involve importing intensively farmed produce from overseas, and the greenhouse emissions this entails are clear. At present, however, a rewilding momentum has been developing and it would be a backward step to slow this down.

D Rewilding holds the promise of seeing once common animals returning to our countryside, to habitats that have been restored. However, one often unrecognised aspect of this is that alongside man-made habitat loss, natural habitats can undergo change independently. This means that a well-intentioned reintroduction might give the animals a home in which they struggle to cope. This note of caution aside, the upsides of rewilding are potentially huge. The financial viability and benefits of well-laid out schemes are rarely in question. For example, restoring forests will aid those areas through increased 'eco-tourism'. In addition, it will enable the absorption of huge quantities of greenhouse gases and so become part of wider climate strategy. Of utmost importance now is a pause: the public are enlightened and receptive, but there is a danger of rushing headlong into a random array of unrelated and potentially incompatible schemes. Therefore, some stock-taking is required.

Which expert

expresses a different opinion from the others regarding whether rewilding can help to limit global warming?

37 ☐

has a similar opinion to C about the pace at which rewilding should occur?

38 ☐

has a similar view to B on how well-informed the general population are about rewilding?

39 ☐

has a different view from the others about the economic benefits of rewilding?

40 ☐

Part 7

You are going to read an article about the sense of smell. Six paragraphs have been removed from the article. Choose from the paragraphs **A–G** the one which fits each gap (**41–46**). There is one extra paragraph which you do not need to use.

Mark your answers **on the separate answer sheet**.

Using our sense of smell

I make perfume for a living, and run workshops at my studio teaching people to recognise different fragrances and produce blends of their own. Even someone who claims to have a terrible sense of smell can become proficient at it.

41	

To do this requires sufficient practice. It's no different from identifying sounds. If you're not a music aficionado, you'll have a hard time distinguishing between a clarinet and an oboe, or a mandolin and a guitar. As you devote attention to listening and spend periods of time watching instruments being played, you begin to improve.

42	

However, it is not just for appreciating beautiful fragrances like these that our sense of smell has been bestowed on us. It evolved for survival: avoiding threats, assessing whether something is edible and identifying people. Most of the time we think we aren't smelling anything at all; we are, but not consciously. That's due to the brain switching off from the signals once it's decided we're safe, although the nose is still picking up scents.

43	

Such effects are demonstrable, but working with perfumes every day, I've found that I can still detect aromas long after untrained noses perceive them as completely gone. It seems it's possible to actually build up our scent stamina.

If we're suffering from tiredness we tend to smell less acutely and less accurately.

44	

To make a very different kind of comparison, consider colour. Working with smell is as varied as working with the colour spectrum, if not more so. But in one particular way, the two are dissimilar. With smell, there's no chart with hundreds of shades to point to so that two people can compare similarities. We're left with a verbal classification system for scent that only keen 'perfumistas' learn.

45	

Another sort of error is feeling certain of your ability to spot the difference between a natural and a synthetic aroma. However, when tested on this, people are generally deceived. For example, lime essential oil is identified by 90% of people as smelling 'chemical'. Yet synthetic but pleasantly smooth lime oxide is almost always identified as natural. Research in neuroscience backs up my observations of this, and it also shows that our ability to smell accurately is affected by stress.

46	

Aside from following sensible advice like that, to continue developing your sense of smell, make it a habit to smell the roses, the coffee, everything you eat. If you smell something nice, stop and identify the source. You'll soon be better at it than you can imagine – and perhaps even as good as a dog!

A Our aroma vocabulary tends to be restricted. In the modern world we struggle to describe scents. Last year I made several futile attempts at creating a perfume for a client who'd requested something deep and heavy. It turned out she had in mind a particular brand that was light and fluffy, but, due to the brand's slightly misleading name, she'd described it as the opposite of what she was seeking.

B One way of dealing with such an issue is for people at my perfume studio who are being taught the art of fragrance recognition to take regular nose breaks, particularly if they're novices, to avoid 'nose blindness'. So, if they can't identify what's on a paper strip, they 'turn off' and then 'turn on' again, as if rebooting a computer.

C In other words, this lack of skill causes a feeling of anxiety instead, which can undermine the ability to detect the odours. Perfume is like any other smell in this respect.

D Despite what many believe, that of humans has the capacity to be on a par with that of dogs and rodents. In fact, we can develop comparable abilities pretty quickly.

E An example of this is when people coming to my studio to learn to create fragrances sometimes put themselves under pressure to produce a masterpiece at their first attempt, and suddenly go frantic, unable to smell anything at all. I tell them to sit down and rest to restore it.

F Perfumers do something similar when we train at specialist colleges. We focus on thousands of odourants sprayed on paper strips until our ability to identify materials by smell alone, as well as detect subtle nuances in quality, has been cultivated. With somewhat less dedication, most people can gain expertise in recognising the finest perfumes.

G This is why the smell of our favourite perfume seems to wear off quickly. Usually it's still there, but we don't need to be reminded about it as it's become familiar. Then, when we step into another environment, our sense of smell checks for danger or food and reports in again, and the seemingly worn-off fragrance briefly returns.

Part 8

You are going to read an article about converting old oil rigs to artificial reef habitats for marine life. For questions **47–56**, choose from the sections (**A–D**). The sections may be chosen more than once.

Mark your answers **on the separate answer sheet**.

In which section does the writer

mention a commercial idea for converting rigs?	**47**	
describe research being carried out at different depths on rigs?	**48**	
say that regulations concerning rigs can be interpreted at a local level?	**49**	
mention an academic overview of environmental rig conversions?	**50**	
mention an environmental reason for not converting rigs?	**51**	
report the difficulty of saying things that are true about all rigs?	**52**	
give details of how rigs are adapted in order to become artificial reefs?	**53**	
highlight a benefit to the rig structure caused by marine life?	**54**	
highlight the problem with taking used rigs back to land?	**55**	
mention that reefs evolving from other structures is not a new phenomenon?	**56**	

Oil rigs may get second lives as fish habitats

Old oil rigs – offshore platforms for oil drilling – can be left on the seabed to become habitats for an abundance of fish and other marine life

A Off the coast of Southern California, USA, a group of aging oil rigs has an uncertain future. After about three to five decades of pumping oil, the rigs are set to be decommissioned. A new study confirms the value of one potential solution: do not tow them to land to be disassembled but let them remain in place to serve as artificial reef habitats for marine life. The study reviews rigs-to-reefs research worldwide, and also contains important new fish surveys conducted on the Californian rigs. It is led by Milton Love, a research biologist at the University of California, Santa Barbara, who has spent three decades assessing the impact of oil rigs on species living nearby. According to Love, there are many different types of rig structures, some mobile, some fixed, depending on various circumstances including water depth. So it can be challenging to make general statements about the ways in which they impact the environment. Regarding the organisms on rigs, he says that there are great similarities and some differences between what you find on a platform and what you find on natural reefs. The water at a depth of 300 to 1,500 meters around rigs acts as nursery grounds, harboring large numbers of juvenile commercial fish like rockfish.

B Love and his colleague Ann Scarborough Bull have both worked on fish counting surveys, where divers descend as far as 30 meters around rigs, following a set path to count and estimate the length of every fish within two meters of themselves. Below 30 meters, researchers use a two-person submarine to perform a similar task: go to the bottom – sometimes 400 meters down – and travel out on the sea floor up to 15 meters around the platform to count all the fish and estimate their size. Love describes the method as the 'gold standard' for doing fish surveys. But it actually produces an underestimate, since the divers only count the fish outside the main structure of the rig. Surprisingly, researchers have found that fish are even more abundant on rigs than on natural reefs nearby, likely because there tends to be less fishing around the rigs. 'It's basically like a marine protected area,' says Bull. Along with juvenile fish, there is an abundance of invertebrates living on the rig – the steel is typically teeming with creatures like mussels, corals, oysters, crabs and shrimps. All that life squeezed onto the steel beams makes the structure slower to rust, adding to its longevity.

C The term 'artificial reefs' is a wide one, covering a broad range of man-made structures which provide ideal habitats for marine life. People have unintentionally been creating artificial reefs for millennia: defensive structures built from wood by Persians and Romans to block the entrance to harbors during wars ended up as rich marine environments. However, the first time artificial reefs were deliberately constructed is thought to have been in 17th-century Japan: rocks were used to grow seaweed and so increase fish numbers. More recently, many decommissioned rigs have been given a new lease of life, in programs around the world. One retired rig off the coast of Borneo has become a new hotel, with four-day dive packages to explore the underwater world.

D Opponents of the rigs-to-reefs idea say that if left, certain types of rig could, over time, leak toxic substances into the water. They therefore support removal of the rigs. But other researchers, including Bull, say that once the rigs are part of a functioning system, it's wise to consider how they impact their surroundings: 'If the platform is completely removed [from the sea], you're also removing all that habitat.' Of course, habitat isn't the only consideration. Rigs impact species on the soft sea floor and they can lower non-fish biodiversity. While governing bodies in the USA advocate the complete removal of rigs after they've been decommissioned, in practice, individual states are typically allowed to make their own decisions. In the Gulf of Mexico, states have transformed 500 rigs into reefs. Energy companies usually remove the upper 25 meters of the rig, which stick out above the water, and recycle it or place it in the water next to the bottom part. Many states may soon have an important choice to make, as rigs near the end of their working lives.

WRITING (1 hour 30 minutes)

Part 1

You **must** answer this question. Write your answer in **220–260** words in an appropriate style **on the separate answer sheet**.

1   Your class has listened to a podcast discussion on students' motivations for studying. You have made the notes below:

Motivations for studying:

- future career
- intellectual curiosity
- improving the world

Some opinions expressed in the discussion:

"Most students want a secure and interesting job."

"A lot of students simply love learning."

"Many students wish to change society for the better."

Write an essay for your tutor discussing **two** of the different motivations for studying in your notes. You should **explain which motivation you think is stronger**, and **provide reasons** to support your answer.

You may, if you wish, make use of the opinions expressed in the discussion, but you should use your own words as far as possible.

Part 2

Write an answer to **one** of the questions **2–4** in this part. Write your answer in **220–260** words in an appropriate style **on the separate answer sheet**. Put the question number in the box at the top of the page.

2   You receive an email from your college principal:

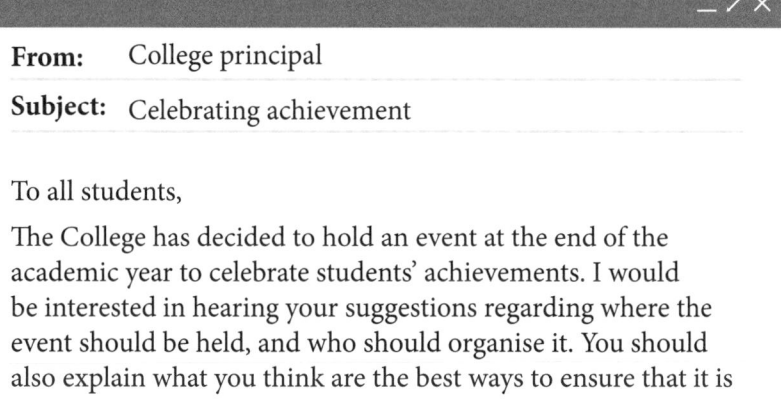

> _ ╱ ×
>
> **From:**   College principal
>
> **Subject:** Celebrating achievement
>
> To all students,
>
> The College has decided to hold an event at the end of the academic year to celebrate students' achievements. I would be interested in hearing your suggestions regarding where the event should be held, and who should organise it. You should also explain what you think are the best ways to ensure that it is an enjoyable and memorable event for the students.

Write your **email**.

3   You see the following announcement on a social media website:

> What are your favourite reality TV programmes? We'd love to know what reality TV programmes people from around the world like. We'd like you to compare two reality TV programmes which are shown in your country, tell us what makes them so popular, and explain which you prefer and why.

Write your **review**.

4   You are a member of an environmental group at an international college and recently the group carried out a project in the local area. Now you've been asked by the principal to write a report on the project for the college website. You should briefly describe the project, evaluate the project's effectiveness and explain how you benefitted from your involvement in it.

Write your **report**.

LISTENING (approximately 40 minutes)

Part 1

Listening test audio

You will hear three different extracts. For questions **1–6**, choose the answer (**A**, **B** or **C**) which fits best according to what you hear. There are two questions for each extract.

Extract One

You hear two friends talking about an article the woman has been reading, all about chairs.

1　As the woman is explaining what the article is about, the man

　　A　expresses interest from the outset.

　　B　is inclined to dismiss the pessimistic tone of it.

　　C　becomes concerned about its implications.

2　What do they agree about the use of chairs through history?

　　A　Chairs have taken on a new significance in certain situations.

　　B　People rejected chairs as being unnecessary at one time.

　　C　The improved designs of chairs made them more user-friendly.

Extract Two

You hear two friends talking about photos of the man's favourite tree.

3　Why is the man so drawn to the tree?

　　A　Its appeal as a meeting point has been to his benefit.

　　B　Its enduring presence has a positive effect on him.

　　C　Its irregular shape particularly attracted him to it.

4　What does the woman say the tree means to her?

　　A　It's allowed her to recall scenes from her childhood.

　　B　It's provided a contrast to unwelcome urban developments.

　　C　It's given her a sense of ownership of a part of her surroundings.

Extract Three

You hear two friends talking about the emergence of new species.

5   What does the man say about new species?

   A   He understands that confirming their existence is complex.

   B   He believes that they are replacing lost ones proportionally.

   C   He thinks there's enough evidence that they evolve fairly quickly.

6   What is the woman doing?

   A   seeking clarification on the subject

   B   opposing the arguments put forward by the man

   C   claiming that the situation is worse than she first thought

Part 2

You will hear a man called Sam Paxton giving a talk to nature-lovers about insects called 'dragonflies'. For questions **7–14**, complete the sentences with a word or short phrase.

Listening test audio

Dragonflies

Sam first became interested in dragonflies on a day when sightings of

(7) .... were scarce.

Sam suggests that (8) .... may be the reason some dragonfly

species in his area were originally lost.

Sam suggests it's mainly because dragonflies are (9) .... that they

are managing to survive.

Sam found that a (10) .... near his home was an excellent place to

observe dragonflies.

Sam feels the word (11) .... best describes the appearance of a

dragonfly's wings.

Sam thinks that distinguishing dragonfly species on the basis of their wing

(12) .... requires expertise.

Because of Sam's fascination with dragonflies, he's recently begun to collect

(13) .... featuring the insects.

Sam says he is giving a talk on (14) .... at his local nature

reserve soon.

Part 3

You will hear an interview in which two palaeontologists, Stella Bersson and Henry Laurent, are talking about their work studying fossils to investigate the history of life on Earth. For questions **15–20**, choose the answer (**A**, **B**, **C** or **D**) which fits best according to what you hear.

Listening test audio

---

15 How does Stella feel about the fact that many dinosaur toys are unrealistic?
    A surprised that they haven't improved over time
    B puzzled by the fact that she didn't spot this as a child
    C frustrated that palaeontologists aren't consulted by toy producers
    D unconcerned as this is what makes them attractive to young children

16 Stella recalls that as she watched a young boy on a TV show, she was
    A amazed by the reaction his performance caused.
    B motivated to become as knowledgeable as he was.
    C shocked at her family's admiration for him.
    B jealous that she couldn't be in his place.

17 In Stella's opinion, a childhood interest in dinosaurs is a positive thing because
    A it encourages children to think about their own origins.
    B it gives children the confidence to disagree with older people.
    C it shows children the value of asking the right questions.
    D it teaches children that there are unanswered questions in science.

18 What point does Henry make about working on the dinosaur film?
    A It was more interesting than the type of work he normally does.
    B He found it difficult to reach a compromise with the director.
    C He didn't feel the need to insist on complete accuracy.
    D It wasn't his job to make the film entertaining.

19 What do Henry and Stella agree on, regarding films featuring dinosaurs?
    A They stimulate public interest in palaeontology.
    B They make a palaeontologist's job more difficult.
    C They should reflect current palaeontological knowledge.
    D They are a source of secret enjoyment for palaeontologists.

20 Henry admits that when palaeontologists give talks to the public, they're often
    A impressed by the sources of information that younger people use.
    B motivated to find out about subjects outside their area of specialisation.
    C nervous that a child will ask about something they have little knowledge of.
    D annoyed by the fact that parents don't encourage their children's interest.

Part 4

Listening test audio

You will hear five short extracts in which people are talking about the book they loved most as a child.

TASK ONE

For questions **21–25**, choose from the list (**A–H**) what each speaker particularly liked about their favourite book as a child.

TASK TWO

For questions **26–30**, choose from the list (**A–H**) how the book still influences each speaker as an adult.

While you listen, you must complete both tasks.

A	the surprising ending
B	the beautiful illustrations
C	the imaginative vocabulary
D	the behaviour of one character
E	the fantasy worlds it revealed
F	the strong relationship it described
G	the outside cover
H	the exciting storyline

Speaker 1	21
Speaker 2	22
Speaker 3	23
Speaker 4	24
Speaker 5	25

A	It's made me better at judging people.
B	It's meant that I'm kinder to others.
C	It reminds me which things are important in life.
D	It affects what I read for pleasure.
E	It's taught me to believe in myself.
F	It's inspired the work I do now.
G	It prevents me from worrying too much.
H	It helps me work out solutions to problems.

Speaker 1	26
Speaker 2	27
Speaker 3	28
Speaker 4	29
Speaker 5	30

Test 3

Icon	What does it mean?
🔊	Listening test audio (Scan the QR code or download from the Resource Bank)

Test 3

READING AND USE OF ENGLISH (1 hour 30 minutes)

Part 1

For questions **1–8**, read the text below and decide which answer (**A, B, C** or **D**) best fits each gap. There is an example at the beginning **(0)**.
Mark your answers **on the separate answer sheet**.

Example:

0   **A** section   **B** class   **C** genre   **D** set

0	A o	B ●	C o	D o

Ancient flying reptiles

Pterosaurs, a **(0)** .... of flying reptiles, evolved from land-based animals. They first **(1)** .... as flying creatures around 245 million years ago, and became extinct 150 million years later, around the same time as dinosaurs. In a new study, scientists have shown how they steadily evolved and became twice as good at flying over the **(2)** .... of their existence.

Fossil records, combined with a new **(3)** .... of flight based on modern birds, were used to measure the reptiles' flight efficiency and to **(4)** .... how they evolved over time. The findings showed their evolution was caused by consistent small improvements over a long period rather than the sudden evolutionary **(5)** .... which had previously been suggested.

Over their 150-million-year history, pterosaurs' body shape and size **(6)** .... to use 50% less energy when flying. They increased in mass by 10 times, with some **(7)** .... weighing more than 300 kg. However, according to the study, there is one group of pterosaurs – azhdarchids – whose flying ability is **(8)** .... to have remained rudimentary in comparison with other pterosaurs.

1	**A** arrived	**B** emerged	**C** encountered	**D** revealed
2	**A** course	**B** term	**C** passage	**D** path
3	**A** version	**B** model	**C** design	**D** imitation
4	**A** enlighten	**B** determine	**C** instruct	**D** dictate
5	**A** leap	**B** blast	**C** spring	**D** flash
6	**A** amended	**B** converted	**C** adapted	**D** conformed
7	**A** conclusively	**B** fundamentally	**C** lastly	**D** ultimately
8	**A** fabled	**B** narrated	**C** famed	**D** reputed

Part 2

For questions **9–16**, read the text below and think of the word which best fits each gap. Use only **one** word in each gap. There is an example at the beginning (**0**).
Write your answers **IN CAPITAL LETTERS on the separate answer sheet**.

Example: | 0 | | T | O | | | | | | | | | | | | | | | | | |

Finding fossilized dinosaur bones

Thanks **(0)** …….. advances in technology, researchers can analyze fossilized dinosaur bones in great detail. However, technology is of much less use when it comes to *finding* fossils. This is largely **(9)** …….. many fossil hunting sites are in remote locations, a fact which **(10)** …….. it impossible for researchers to transport ground-penetrating radar machinery there. Even in areas where machinery could eventually be transported, the costs in time and money usually rule this **(11)** …….. as an option.

Supposing radar did detect **(12)** …….. might be an interesting object, researchers may end up deciding not to proceed with any excavations anyway. They would have to consider **(13)** …….. the object was likely to be interesting **(14)** …….. to be worth the effort. After all, there are often plenty of fossils visible at the surface.

Therefore, it is keen eyesight scientists rely on, **(15)** …….. opposed to high-tech equipment. The best fossil hunters can even spot tiny bits of fossilized bone in rock, in **(16)** …….. of the fact that rock and fossil are often similar in color and texture.

Part 3

For questions **17–24**, read the text below. Use the word given in capitals at the end of some of the lines to form a word that fits in the gap **in the same line**. There is an example at the beginning (**0**). Write your answers **IN CAPITAL LETTERS on the separate answer sheet**.

Example:

| 0 | B | E | N | E | F | I | C | I | A | L | | | | | | | |

The advantages of outdoor learning

I, like all teachers, had heard about the (**0**) …….. effects of outdoor learning for children. But it wasn't something I gave much thought to; I engaged with it when required to do so but without much understanding or (**17**) …….. . However, moving recently to a (**18**) …….. new school, where outdoor learning is given much greater priority, has changed my (**19**) …….. entirely.

BENEFIT

ENTHUSE
PROGRESS
LOOK

Often, children who struggle more within the (**20**) …….. of the classroom flourish in outdoor spaces, where they feel more independent. This (**21**) …….. exploration and creativity to take place in new ways. Outdoor learning also gives them opportunities to offer ideas spontaneously rather than always as a (**22**) …….. to the teacher's questions.

RESTRICT

ABLE

RESPOND

With outdoor learning I see my class in a different light. Children's behaviour can shift, and differences between pupils that may have been apparent in the classroom might not be so outside. If other teachers are, as I was, a little (**23**) …….. at first, then I would urge them to throw themselves into outdoor learning! It will be a (**24**) …….. rewarding experience!

HESITATE

MASS

Part 4

For questions **25–30**, complete the second sentence so that it has a similar meaning to the first sentence, using the word given. **Do not change the word given**. You must use between **three** and **six** words, including the word given. Here is an example (**0**).

Example:

0   James would only speak to the head of department alone.

ON

James .... to the head of department alone.

The gap can be filled with the words 'insisted on speaking', so you write

| **Example:** | **0** | *INSISTED ON SPEAKING* |

Write **only** the missing words **IN CAPITAL LETTERS on the separate answer sheet**.

---

25   As well as playing very stylishly, Tom also hit some powerful shots during the match.

PLAY

Not .... great style, but he also hit some powerful shots during the match.

26   Although Julia didn't get a demonstration of the new software, she managed to do what she wanted with it.

SHOWN

Despite not .... to use the new software, Julia managed to do what she wanted with it.

27   A lot of people oppose the plans to knock down these old buildings.

DEAL

There's .... the plans to knock down these old buildings.

28 'I'll do the presentation if you give me sufficient time to prepare,' said David.

CONDITION

David agreed to do the presentation …………………………..... given sufficient time to prepare.

29 People believe that this opera company's best singer is on the point of retiring.

ABOUT

This opera company's best singer is believed …………………………..... retire.

30 The manager told his team that they shouldn't assume that they'd easily win the match.

GRANTED

The manager told his team not …………………………..... that they'd easily win the match.

Part 5

You are going to read an article about a museum. For questions **31–36**, choose the answer (**A**, **B**, **C** or **D**) which you think fits best according to the text.

Mark your answers **on the separate answer sheet**.

Depot

Rotterdam's major art museum has just completed an additional building, called Depot

In the centre of Rotterdam, there's a building called Depot which, from a block away, looks like something from a more advanced civilisation. Its futuristic, mirrored glass walls curve up 40 metres, reflecting the iron-grey clouds and fractured city skyline. This city's residents are used to cutting-edge architecture, but it's not, as a rule, seen in storage facilities which is, after all, what the word 'depot' implies. When I went to visit it, a couple of Rotterdammers were debating whether they liked it. They decided not, but snapped selfies in front of it anyway.

Depot was created as a home for artefacts belonging to the Boijmans Van Beuningen museum not currently displayed in its main building. To call it a warehouse is, however, to do it a considerable injustice. This isn't just a storage facility, but an attempt to let the public have some access to all the artworks the museum possesses. Instead of locking a large proportion of its prized artefacts away behind closed doors, the Boijmans has ploughed €55 million into this project. As I met him at the entrance, Sjarel Ex, the museum's director, gestured towards the network of glass stairwells above our heads and proudly explained that every single item the museum owned could be accommodated there.

Seven years ago, the Boijmans' basement vaults – the old storage area – flooded. Though damage was minimal, it was obvious the museum needed to upgrade, particularly as 90% of Rotterdam is below sea level. But instead of erecting something anonymous far from the city centre, Ex opted for a high-profile location. 'So much of what museums do happens in the dark. We wanted to bring some of it into the light.' There were already plans to close the main building for seven years for renovation, so the new building also helped bridge this gap.

Despite being open to the public, the conditions in Depot are as good if not better than in a regular storage facility: high-grade air conditioning keeps the environment dust-free, and there are five 'climate zones' for different kinds of artefacts. While some pieces are on movable racks or in display cabinets, light-sensitive objects are kept in sealed cabinets and can only be inspected by appointment. Ex didn't go into detail about security, but assured me that the building was more than a match for art thieves.

However, most museums don't have the resources to build such new facilities. Some people also suspect that, eye-catching as visible-storage projects are, they're more of a symbolic than a real change to the way museums operate. Furthermore, does anyone have the appetite to see the 2.3 million artefacts owned by London's Victoria and Albert Museum? Or the Smithsonian's 155 million across 19 institutions in the USA? Where would you even start? Isn't that what curators are for? When I raise these points with Ex, he nods. 'Sure. Projects like ours are an experiment. Will anyone come? Or will they come to Depot, and not to the beautifully curated exhibitions in the museum?' He shrugs. 'We'll see.'

A train ride across the Netherlands from Rotterdam, Amsterdam's Rijksmuseum is attempting its own version of radical transparency. The museum's most famous painting, Rembrandt's *The Night Watch*, is currently encased in a giant glass box. Conservators work inside while members of the public watch. Rijksmuseum's director, Taco Dibbits, concedes that locking it in the conservation studio for years wasn't realistic – it's the reason most people visit the museum. Restoring it on display has benefits, too. 'For museums, the way forward is how you share research,' he suggests. 'We sometimes underestimate how fascinated the public is.' For both Dibbits and Ex, opening up marks a shift in the way museums see their role. 'We have to think much harder about transparency if we want to survive,' remarks Ex. Dibbits concurs. 'The objects stay the same,' he says. 'But how we talk about and show them – that really has to keep changing.'

31 What does the writer suggest about Depot in the first paragraph?

    A There has been some local resistance to its construction.
    B There is a mismatch between its appearance and its function.
    C Its modern style is inappropriate for the city.
    D It looks better when viewed from a distance.

32 In the second paragraph, the writer points out that Depot

    A has given the museum the chance to re-evaluate its policies.
    B has the capacity to house the museum's entire collection.
    C is a confusing place to find your way around.
    D is worth the money that was spent on it.

33 For Sjarel Ex, a significant factor in the decision to build Depot was a desire

    A to reduce the effects of water damage in part of the museum.
    B to shorten the length of time the museum needed to close for.
    C to increase public awareness of how the museum operates.
    D to avoid overcrowding in the main museum building.

34 In the fourth paragraph, the writer explains how Depot

    A creates a pleasant atmosphere for staff and visitors.
    B displays its artefacts in an innovative way.
    C ensures that nothing can be stolen.
    D prevents items from deteriorating.

35 What point is the writer making about open storage in the fifth paragraph?

    A Other museums want to see whether it works before trying it.
    B The expense means it can't ever be more than a publicity stunt.
    C It is unlikely to be as beneficial as it sounds in theory.
    D It could lead to museum employees losing their jobs.

36 Why does the writer mention the Rijksmuseum in Amsterdam in this article about the Boijmans?

    A Public opinion on the role of museums is similar in both cities.
    B It has a similar objective but with a different type of project.
    C Public reaction to its latest proposals has been similar.
    D The changes it is making are occurring in a similar time frame.

Part 6

You are going to read four extracts from articles in which literary critics give their views on authors self-publishing their work. For questions **37–40**, choose from the literary critics **A–D**. The literary critics may be chosen more than once.

Mark your answers **on the separate answer sheet**.

Authors self-publishing their work

A Constantin Dinu

It's never been easier to self-publish a book you've written. The fact that self-published work rarely, if ever, makes the bestseller lists, however, is testament to the widespread scepticism about its quality. Without experienced publishing-house professionals to beat mediocre work into something resembling a readable book, it stays mediocre despite the best efforts of its author. Self-publishing is the perfect means for anyone who has more interest in seeing their name on the cover of a book than in creating critically respected literature to achieve their dream, but no one I'm aware of has ever been able to sustain a living through self-publishing alone. I suspect this is not simply a reflection of the quality, but also of the author's lack of promotional know-how. Sticking some information about it on social media, which is apparently what the majority do, will never turn you into a household name.

B Hideko Tamura

Long gone are the days when the only people who would ever consider self-publishing were those whose main aim was to boast about being a published author. Many established writers who have already published work through the traditional route are now turning to it. They have realised that they can earn substantially more without publishing houses taking a cut, which is also surely true for new and lesser-known authors if they are sufficiently talented and their work is meticulously checked and corrected, which alas still isn't always the case. Public cynicism at the merit of much self-published work has largely evaporated, thanks to several extremely well-written, high-profile novels. Self-published writers may not share the expertise of traditional publishers when it comes to generating sales through advertising and so on, but access to how best to do it is becoming increasingly available online, so this situation is rapidly changing.

C Helena Silveira

Self-publishing is inevitably on the rise, thanks largely to the internet. It now makes up around 10% of published work, and people are cottoning onto the fact that a reasonable proportion of it is actually of an increasingly high standard. One major reason for this is that authors have realised that writing something then immediately publishing it without getting others to read it and suggest improvements is not the way to go. They have therefore enlisted trusted friends or family to take on this essential role, leading to a higher-quality end product. I'm sure sales figures for self-published titles would be higher were it not for authors' lack of expertise when it comes to publicising their work. This generally disappointing performance has meant that many dreams of being able to afford to become a full-time writer as a result of self-publishing have largely been shattered, which is a shame.

D Richard French

The standard of a significant quantity of self-published writing these days is comparable with much traditionally published work. Despite this, reader confidence in how good self-published work is remains frighteningly low. Most self-published writers now understand that a great deal of work must go into getting a book from first-draft stage to something worthy of being published. They have invested more time into this and sought help from others to bring it about. The results are generally impressive. However, creating publicity for their work continues to be an area that requires considerable improvement and until this issue is addressed, self-publishing will continue to generate insufficient income for many authors to survive without also taking on other work. While self-publication might have once been purely a means for bad writers to get their name in print, perhaps the fact that it is today used by many serious writers will help increase sales.

Which critic

shares a view with D about the current reputation of self-published books?

37	

has a different view to the others about the financial implications for writers self-publishing a book?

38	

shares an opinion with C about the effectiveness of the editing process for self-published books?

39	

has a different view to the others about how well marketing of self-published books is typically done?

40	

Part 7

You are going to read an article about a musician playing a unique violin. Six paragraphs have been removed from the article. Choose from the paragraphs **A–G** the one which fits each gap (**41–46**). There is one extra paragraph which you do not need to use.

Mark your answers **on the separate answer sheet**.

In dialogue with Mozart

Musician Christoph Koncz has used Mozart's violin when recording the 18th-century composer's five violin concertos

The house where Wolfgang Amadeus Mozart was born is now a museum in Salzburg, Austria, called the Mozarteum. When the musician Christoph Koncz went there and dared to ask the keepers of Mozart's violin if he might be allowed to try it out, he had no idea where the question would lead. Astonishingly, they left him alone with it in a room, and closed the door. He played non-stop for several hours.

41	

Eight years later, after hundreds of hours of practice on the gut-stringed Baroque instrument, Koncz has produced the first ever recording of Mozart's five violin concertos on the very same violin on which the musical genius composed them between 1773 and 1775. Mozart also almost certainly performed them on the instrument. 'It's a museum instrument,' says Koncz, 'but we musicians believe an instrument only has one purpose: to be played. I have been allowed to bring it to life again.'

42	

Koncz says that the recordings he has now made are vital for sharing something very close to what Mozart would have heard. 'They take this sound, which only a few people would otherwise get to hear, beyond the concert hall. I draw huge inspiration from the fact that the sound I produce on the violin is probably very similar to something that Mozart heard in his own ear.' Probably the first full-sized violin to be owned by Mozart, it was built in the mid 18th century in Mittenwald in Bavaria, a town still famous for its violin making. It is believed to have been given to him by his father, Leopold, his sole violin tutor.

43	

Koncz plays the violin without a shoulder rest, which requires a different style of playing to that commonly used nowadays. And, unusually, the violin itself has not been modernised. Koncz says it is extraordinary that the main parts of Mozart's violin are all in their original condition.

44	

The violin passed from Mozart to his sister Nannerl, a piano teacher, when he moved to Vienna at the age of 25. After Mozart's untimely death at 35, one of Nannerl's star pupils purchased the instrument.

45	

The five concertos Koncz has recorded are a mainstay of any classical violinist's repertoire. They progress in complexity and sophistication and, says Koncz, are a record of the speed with which Mozart developed as a musician.

46	

In one of the most challenging parts of his project, Koncz set about composing his own. He tried to remain true to Mozart by studying the surviving ones he had written for his keyboard concertos, composing them for others to play. 'It's like being in dialogue with him, over the centuries, trying to imagine what he would have done at this point, at the same time as feeling a huge responsibility. It kept me awake at times.'

A However, there is an obvious explanation: 'Due to its association with him it was recognised early on how precious this instrument is and nobody dared to actually change it,' says Koncz, who has carried out extensive research into its history.

B Doing so required a great deal of time and effort. 'As it was very rarely played, at first its wood was stiff, it lacked resonance and its sound had fallen asleep. I played it for hours and days at a time and each time I played it, its sound opened up and the wood was in harmony again. The time it took to get it into shape each day became shorter the more often I played it.'

C Despite those reservations, they knew there might never be a better opportunity. For Koncz and those behind the project, it therefore felt like a fitting moment to bring an instrument that had been mainly confined to a glass display case to a wider audience.

D Over the following years, the violin changed hands several more times. Then, in 1956, it was acquired by the Mozarteum, the leading foundation dedicated to preserving the musician's legacy.

E Mozart would have played on it when he became concert master at the Salzburg Hofkapelle at the age of 13. While on tour in 1777, he wrote to him about playing his second concerto on the violin, 'everyone praised my beautiful, pure tone'.

F 'It was blissful, an awakening. I'm pretty convinced no one since Mozart had spent so much time on it,' Koncz says. He adds that every time he has picked the violin up since that day, he feels as if he is communicating directly with Mozart himself.

G What he did not leave behind, however, was a score for the cadenzas, the ornamental passages within each piece allowing solo players to show off their skills. This is another clue that Mozart performed the violin pieces himself, Koncz says, and that he probably improvised these cadenzas.

Part 8

You are going to read an article about a fastener for footwear and clothing known as Velcro. For questions **47–56**, choose from the sections (**A–D**). The sections may be chosen more than once. Mark your answers **on the separate answer sheet**.

In which section does the writer

highlight the fact that Velcro was adopted in a wide range of fields?	47
point out that Velcro's unappealing qualities have not stopped it being a noteworthy development?	48
mention a fashion item using Velcro that has been frequently displayed to the public?	49
consider how Velcro might be rated on its attractiveness compared to alternatives?	50
speculate on why Velcro failed to achieve approval from many consumers?	51
explain the mechanics behind the concept of Velcro?	52
describe a change in how Velcro was generally viewed?	53
claim that Velcro stimulated the imagination of some artistic people?	54
talk about Velcro being used in particularly momentous circumstances?	55
mention an example of business responding to a consumer's request?	56

The story of Velcro as a fastener

A Hold a magnifying glass to the fastener Velcro and you'll find that it's essentially a strip of fabric covered with a ton of teeny-tiny hooks that are somehow miraculously attached temporarily to another strip with even tinier loops. If we were to rank clothing fasteners such as buttons, zips, hooks, toggles and ties on their chicness or discreetness or glamour, Velcro would probably come in last. That grating 'chshshhhh' sound alone is enough to turn off the majority of us. But it's hard to ignore the fact that it's an invention that forever changed the landscape of fashion. The idea for Velcro dawned on Swiss electrical engineer George de Mestral in 1941 when, during a hike through the woods, he wondered why bits of the prickly weed burdock clung to his dog's fur. He studied them closely and, after experimenting with various materials, eventually patented his brainchild – the hook-and-loop system – in 1955, naming it Velcro, a blend of the French words velour ('velvet') and crochet ('hook').

B The response was overwhelming. In 1958, columnist Sylvia Porter was given the opportunity to preview the invention. 'The new fastening device is in many ways potentially more revolutionary than was the zipper a quarter-century ago,' she wrote. A year later, another journalist said of Velcro, 'the big noise this spring will be a sound like ripping cloth.' And revolutionary it was. From the outset, its use was rooted in utilitarianism, and it rapidly replaced other fasteners for securing solar panels or holding pieces of AstroTurf together. On the clothing front, it was praised for its swift, easy-on, easy-off convenience for those whose professions relied on speed: the military, firefighters, athletes and so on. Most famously, Velcro was chosen to secure Neil Armstrong's space suit for the first ever walk on the moon in 1969.

C Several visionary couturiers played with the new material and conjured it into one-of-a-kind looks. In the 60s, fashion designer Paco Rabanne experimented with it, along with adhesive tape, metal discs and chains, in his outlandish creations. Influenced by futurism and modernism, André Courrèges unveiled a space-inspired collection in 1964 with crisp, geometric dresses crafted out of unlikely textiles, including Velcro, nylon tape, plastic and vinyl. The accompanying white boots – a square peep-toe that fastened up the centre with Velcro – became one of his most enduring designs, forever immortalised in numerous exhibitions of the history of fashion. Velcro's ease of use was repeatedly lauded. In 2012, Matthew Walzer, a teenager with cerebral palsy, wrote a letter to footwear, accessories and clothing multinational Nike appealing for a fashionable sneaker he could put on without assistance. This inspired the sportswear giant to work on a new line of sneakers. 'One of the key learnings we've had ... is the importance of easy entry and exit of the shoe, not just simplifying its fastening system,' said a senior director. Nike's Velcro-strapped FlyEase caught on with athletes of all abilities.

D Yet, despite all these advances and the handful of placements in couture collections, Velcro in high fashion never really took off. Early memories of Velcro-strapped shoes from the toddler years might be a reason. And functional footwear that defined the 80s and 90s, which incorporated Velcro to secure the foot, was a far cry from sleek stilettos. It really wasn't until practical shoes with chunky soles and Velcro fasteners were not only embraced by the fashion world, but also catapulted into mainstream fame that, all of a sudden, Velcro was no longer uncool. It pervaded the street-style scene of subsequent fashion collections, and then a new sneaker movement saw designer labels introducing Velcro versions of signature styles. When one celebrity donned a black lace-trimmed dress with a pair of white Velcro sneakers for a major fashion event, it made headlines. And while Velcro is still most prominently seen in the sneaker world, there have been notable instances of it making its way into high street clothing retailing due to trends towards highly practical ways of dressing.

WRITING (1 hour 30 minutes)

Part 1

You **must** answer this question. Write your answer in **220–260** words in an appropriate style **on the separate answer sheet**.

---

1   Your class has listened to an online discussion about why young people should study business at school. You have made the notes below:

> ### Why young people should study business at school:
>
> - increased opportunities for jobs
> - better workplace communication skills
> - more understanding of money

> **Some opinions expressed in the discussion:**
>
> "Relevant qualifications give you an advantage in the job market."
>
> "In today's fast-moving world, businesses need to exchange information quickly and accurately."
>
> "Being able to manage your finances when you leave education is very useful."

Write an essay for your tutor discussing **two** of the ideas in your notes about why young people should study business at school. You should **explain which idea you think is more important** and **give reasons justifying** your opinion.

You may, if you wish, make use of the opinions expressed in the discussion, but you should use your own words as far as possible.

Part 2

Write an answer to **one** of the questions **2–4** in this part. Write your answer in **220–260** words in an appropriate style **on the separate answer sheet**. Put the question number in the box at the top of the page.

---

2   You are a volunteer at an international summer school for young children. The director of the summer school has asked for suggestions about how to help the children learn more about food, and you have decided to submit a proposal. You should briefly describe two activities that could help the children to learn more about food, explaining why you think these activities would be particularly effective.

Write your **proposal**.

3   You see this advertisement on a music website:

> ### International music bloggers wanted
>
> Calling all music lovers around the world! Could you write a blog for our website?
>
> If you're interested in writing a blog for our website, then email me, Amy Venn.
>
> Please tell me what your own interest in music is, what aspects of the music scene in your country you could write about, and why you think your blog will appeal to our readers. You should also mention whether you have any other relevant writing experience.

Write your **email**.

4   You recently saw a programme about nature that made a strong impression on you. Write a review of the programme for a website about TV programmes. Explain how you felt after watching the programme. Comment on the extent to which you think the nature programme achieved its aims and suggest an idea for a future programme with a similar aim.

Write your **review**.

LISTENING (approximately 40 minutes)

Part 1

You will hear three different extracts. For questions **1–6**, choose the answer (**A**, **B** or **C**) which fits best according to what you hear. There are two questions for each extract.

Listening test audio

Extract One

You hear part of a discussion between a jewellery designer and a retailer.

1   What does the woman say her focus is when she's designing jewellery?

   A   expressing her personal tastes

   B   maintaining her standards

   C   becoming more widely known

2   How does the man feel about selling jewellery?

   A   keen to change the attitude of consumers

   B   anxious about the current state of the market

   C   irritated by losing business to bigger retailers

Extract Two

You hear two actors who voice the characters in video games talking about their work.

3   What does the woman love about voicing characters in video games?

   A   the particular challenges it involves

   B   the considerable benefits it brings

   C   the feedback she gets from games players

4   When talking about his work, the man

   A   clarifies the reasons he does it.

   B   identifies some of its disadvantages.

   C   suggests improvements to certain aspects of it.

Extract Three

You hear two psychologists discussing some research into complaining.

5   When talking about the research into complaining, the man

   A   illustrates one of its theories.

   B   explains why it was necessary.

   C   questions its objectivity.

6   What do they agree causes people to decide to complain?

   A   a particular level of frustration

   B   a desire to profit from a situation

   C   a generally pessimistic attitude to life

Part 2

You will hear a British student called Talya Evesham giving a talk to fellow students about the year she spent in South Africa as part of her degree in zoology. For questions **7–14**, complete the sentences with a word or short phrase.

Listening test audio

My research trip to South Africa

Talya found the **(7)** .... the most difficult aspect of her stay at the

Succulent Karoo Research Station.

Talya was grateful for the level of **(8)** .... that her tutor gave her for her

research project.

Talya studied the **(9)** .... of a small mammal called a bush Karoo rat.

The scientists at the research station taught Talya how to attach

(10) .... to bush Karoo rats.

Talya says that assessing the bush Karoo rats' **(11)** .... in the

laboratory was a particularly memorable experience.

Talya carried out some **(12)** .... in order to help out another

undergraduate.

Talya feels that the experience she gained of coping with **(13)** ....

will be of particular interest to future employers.

Talya has now decided that she'd like to do a postgraduate course in

(14) .... when she finishes her first degree.

Part 3

Listening test audio

You will hear part of an interview with two pianists, Angela Gransom and Carl Avering, talking about the state of classical music. For questions **15–20**, choose the answer (**A**, **B**, **C** or **D**) which fits best according to what you hear.

15 Carl believes that the decline in the number of people who play musical instruments is a result of
   A people preferring more passive pastimes.
   B instruments being viewed as too expensive.
   C a change in attitude towards inheriting things.
   D families having no interest in musical education.

16 What does Angela think about the benefits of learning music in school?
   A It lowers aggressive tendencies in the young.
   B It helps develop better cognitive skills.
   C It gives students a more balanced curriculum.
   D It provides students with a wider range of career choices.

17 Angela says the diminishing size of audiences for classical concerts is mainly due to
   A a decline in the technical abilities of modern performers.
   B a reluctance to fit lengthy concerts into busy lives.
   C the growth in alternative forms of entertainment.
   D the spread of classical music into all areas of day-to-day life.

18 Carl and Angela both say that to get more people going to classical concerts,
   A a wider range of new music needs to be composed.
   B performers need to adopt more engaging approaches.
   C the broadcast media need to give more airtime to music.
   D the views of a broader cross-section of society need to be considered.

19 What does Carl say about touring?
   A He appreciates his interaction with a range of people.
   B He resents having to cope with poor equipment.
   C He is fascinated by the local musicians he observes.
   D He finds the whole process rather exhausting.

20 How does Carl respond when asked about the issue of ageing audiences?
   A He rejects what he believes is a mistaken view.
   B He criticises the organisers of classical music performances.
   C He acknowledges the urgency of finding a solution.
   D He applauds the efforts most educators are making.

Listening test audio

Part 4

You will hear five short extracts in which people are talking about the language course they attend.

TASK ONE

For questions **21–25**, choose from the list (**A–H**) the reason each speaker gives for attending the language course.

TASK TWO

For questions **26–30**, choose from the list (**A–H**) what each speaker dislikes about the language course.

While you listen, you must complete both tasks.

TASK ONE		TASK TWO	
A	to feel closer to relatives	A	the pace of individual lessons
B	to enable a career change	B	the time needed for studying
C	to be mentally stimulated	C	the physical demands
D	to form new relationships	D	the particular teaching methods
E	to pass on knowledge to colleagues	E	the behaviour of some participants
F	to move to a new country	F	the learning materials provided
G	to gain cultural awareness	G	the focus on regional variations
H	to act as a role model for peers		

Speaker 1	21
Speaker 2	22
Speaker 3	23
Speaker 4	24
Speaker 5	25

Speaker 1	26
Speaker 2	27
Speaker 3	28
Speaker 4	29
Speaker 5	30

Test 4

Icon	What does it mean?
🔊	Listening test audio (Scan the QR code or download from the Resource Bank)

Test 4

READING AND USE OF ENGLISH (1 hour 30 minutes)

Part 1

For questions **1–8**, read the text below and decide which answer (**A, B, C** or **D**) best fits each gap. There is an example at the beginning (**0**).
Mark your answers **on the separate answer sheet**.

Example:

0 **A** originated   **B** embarked   **C** launched   **D** sprang

0	A ○	B ○	C ●	D ○

Tiger sculpture sparks armed police response

Police in Kent, UK, recently **(0)** …….. an urgent response to reports of a large wild cat spotted in the area. Armed officers, and even a helicopter, were **(1)** …….. following a call from a member of the public, who had caught sight of a tiger while walking near the village of Underriver. However, the animal **(2)** …….. out to be a life-size sculpture created by artist Juliet Simpson.

On hearing that police were investigating a tiger on the **(3)** …….. , Ms Simpson set off towards her statue. 'Out of the field opposite came a whole crowd of armed police, who by then knew that it was all a false alarm.' The artwork, which had **(4)** …….. the same spot close to a footpath for over 20 years, was designed to look realistic. **(5)** …….. , it had never previously been reported as **(6)** …….. a threat to the public.

Police confirmed that armed officers had attended the scene as a **(7)** …….. and, following a search of the area, had **(8)** …….. that there was no risk to the public.

1   **A** put forward   **B** drawn on   **C** taken up   **D** brought in

2   **A** turned   **B** ended   **C** came   **D** got

3   **A** clear   **B** open   **C** loose   **D** free

4   **A** occupied   **B** stood   **C** remained   **D** stayed

5   **A** Therefore   **B** Otherwise   **C** Hence   **D** Nonetheless

6   **A** staging   **B** offering   **C** posing   **D** triggering

7   **A** security   **B** precaution   **C** defence   **D** protection

8   **A** settled   **B** exposed   **C** authorised   **D** established

Part 2

For questions **9–16**, read the text below and think of the word which best fits each gap. Use only **one** word in each gap. There is an example at the beginning (**0**).
Write your answers **IN CAPITAL LETTERS on the separate answer sheet**.

Example: | 0 | | C | A | M | E | | | | | | | | | | | | | |

ÅBEN online platform

The inspiration for his online platform called ÅBEN **(0)** …….. to David Harrigan when he was decorating his own home. Browsing the internet **(9)** …….. search of work by Scandinavian interior designers, he could find **(10)** …….. single site able to meet his needs. His frustration was **(11)** …….. sparked the idea for the platform, which puts Scandinavian designers in touch with consumers who are on the lookout for custom-made furniture, glassware or ceramics. On the **(12)** …….. hand, ÅBEN helps consumers find products that aren't mass-produced, whilst giving budding designers a shop window on the other.

ÅBEN's platform works **(13)** …….. any other e-shop, but with a personal twist. Once a customer has purchased an item through the website, David gives the designer a call to ascertain how long production will take. In order to make a unique piece **(14)** …….. scratch, the designer needs time, **(15)** …….. keen customers are to get a delivery. As long as David makes the customer **(16)** …….. of this in advance, everything works out fine.

Part 3

For questions **17–24**, read the text below. Use the word given in capitals at the end of some of the lines to form a word that fits in the gap **in the same line**. There is an example at the beginning (**0**). Write your answers **IN CAPITAL LETTERS on the separate answer sheet**.

Example: | 0 | I | N | V | E | N | T | I | O | N | | | | | | | | | |

Single-use objects are nothing new

Many people probably consider throwaway coffee cups to be a
modern (**0**) …….. . However, the Minoans, one of the first advanced   **INVENT**
civilisations in Europe, were making single-use cups 3,500 years
ago. Their disposable pottery cups were popular at large social
(**17**) …….. for the chance they offered the hosts to display their   **GATHER**
wealth and (**18**) …….. .   **SOPHISTICATED**

At a recent museum exhibition designed to show the (**19**) …….. of   **EXTEND**
plastic pollution, one of the Minoan cups was displayed alongside
modern single-use objects. The (**20**) …….. of the ancient cup   **INCLUDE**
among the more recent items was deliberately thought-provoking.
The curators' aim was to make visitors consider their (**21**) ……..   **RELATE**
with waste, and to think creatively about reducing the amount they
produce. They hoped that this would prove more (**22**) …….. than   **FRUIT**
making people feel guilty. As one curator points out, for humans,
generating waste is simply (**23**) …….. . Our use of tools, clothes   **AVOID**
and other items which wear out means that it is in the nature of our
(**24**) …….. to throw things away.   **EXIST**

Part 4

For questions **25–30**, complete the second sentence so that it has a similar meaning to the first sentence, using the word given. **Do not change the word given**. You must use between **three** and **six** words, including the word given. Here is an example (**0**).

Example:

0   My brother now earns far less than he did when he was younger.

NEARLY

My brother ………………………………… much now as he did when he was younger.

The gap can be filled with the words 'does not earn nearly as', so you write:

Example:	0	*DOES NOT EARN NEARLY AS*

Write **only** the missing words **IN CAPITAL LETTERS on the separate answer sheet**.

---

25   Diana was supposed to have replied to my email by last Friday.

OUGHT

There ………………………………..... a reply from Diana to my email by last Friday.

26   Richard decided to open his sister's mail while she was away on holiday.

LIBERTY

Richard ………………………………..... his sister's mail while she was away on holiday.

27   The owner insisted that the company's poor performance wasn't his fault.

BLAME

The owner refused ………………………………..... the company's poor performance.

28 If nobody objects, the meeting will be postponed until next Tuesday.

THERE

As ………………………………….... objections, the meeting will be postponed until next Tuesday.

29 'Antisocial behaviour like this really can't go on,' said the Head Teacher.

STOP

'We really need to put …………………………………... of antisocial behaviour,' said the Head Teacher.

30 The police accused Peter of committing a serious crime.

ALLEGED

Peter …………………………………... a serious crime by the police.

Part 5

You are going to read an article about financial literacy. For questions **31–36**, choose the answer (**A**, **B**, **C** or **D**) which you think fits best according to the text.
Mark your answers **on the separate answer sheet**.

The importance of financial literacy

Everybody needs to have a grasp of basic finance in today's society

Growing up in an unremarkable small town in industrial South Wales, with a music teacher dad and a psychologist mum, there weren't many signs to suggest that I'd take up a career in finance. Then, for my 16th birthday, my father gave me a present: £100-worth of shares in a large national utility company that had just been privatised. I'm still in the dark as to what prompted that gesture. I was hardly a star pupil when it came to maths, but for me it marked a turning point. For months afterwards, I'd check the share-price pages of the daily newspaper. If the stock was up a ½ pence, I'd rejoice that I was much better off. Primitive stuff. And yet that early interest has taken me to my current job as a financial consultant, and financial literacy has been the cornerstone of my career.

The contrast between my professional life and the realities of everyday life in northeast London where I now live, with its stark gap between the haves and have-nots, is among the factors that have led me to try to make a difference. In the coming months, I'm going to have a role in the establishment of a charitable foundation aimed at improving financial literacy. We no longer live in a world where the approachable staff at the local bank represent the average person's only point of contact with the world of finance. The shift towards a bewildering choice of financial products, self-determined retirement planning and easy credit for impulse buys on the internet all combine to make a firm grasp of basic finance a fundamental necessity of life, and it affects people of all generations: your mobile phone contract might be great value or a horrible rip-off. Needless to say, there's no shortage of unscrupulous operators out there ready to exploit the unwary. All of these are reasons enough to be launching this initiative, and what better time than the present to do so.

To my shame, I hadn't been back to my old school in the years since I left. But I was determined to find out what the current generation of students felt about their financial futures, and it seemed like the right place to start. In a brief question-and-answer session, I was predictably asked about topics like student loans, and for advice on how to break into the job market. The questions from the final-year students were smart, and revealed a genuine level of concern regarding the economic state of the country, but few touched on the realm of personal finance. Where they did, the questions struck me as fairly basic given that financial literacy is being promoted in schools across the country nowadays. In practice, provision is patchy – as in much of the world – and this could well be the reason.

It seems there is even less to engage this generation in the practicalities of basic personal finance than was the case in my day. Teenagers make up one of the groups in society which the financial literacy foundation plans to focus on. People in each of the groups identified have been shown by academic research to fall below average levels of understanding in basic finance, increasing the likelihood that they will be unable to budget efficiently, will get into unsustainable debt or will be open to exploitation.

The charitable foundation aims to create a series of educational videos and other material, and will be collaborating with existing charities to distribute them at national level. Industry professionals will be invited to contribute both financially and as volunteers to help promote the cause. Andy Haldane, the former Bank of England chief economist and vice-chair of the National Numeracy Campaign, which promotes everyday maths skills, is hoping that the charity will be able to channel financial expertise, particularly that of the major financial institutions in the capital, for the greater good. 'What a shame it is that we have a huge repository of financial literacy in one tiny part of the country and huge need for it everywhere else,' he says. 'We want to spread some of that knowledge.'

31 The writer's father bought her shares in a company
  A to encourage her unexpected interest in finance.
  B for reasons that remain unclear to her even now.
  C as it reflected the subjects she was studying at the time.
  D because he could see that she had a real talent for figures.

32 The writer has chosen to participate in the financial literacy project partly as a result of
  A other voluntary activities she's been involved in.
  B witnessing some social inequalities at first hand.
  C work that she's been doing in her local community.
  D a wish to help young people who come to her for advice.

33 In the second paragraph, the writer makes the point that people today
  A are expected to take greater responsibility for financial decisions.
  B benefit from a wider range of financial products on the market.
  C are more likely than ever to fall victim to criminal activities.
  D are becoming vulnerable to financial problems at a younger age.

34 What made an impression on the writer when she visited students in her old school?
  A how concerned they were about certain key issues
  B how little things had changed since her own time there
  C how uninformed they were about current affairs in general
  D how ineffective one educational initiative seemed to have been

35 The writer mentions academic research in the fourth paragraph to support her point that
  A aspects of financial planning should be taught in all schools.
  B adults will probably benefit most from help with financial planning.
  C help with financial planning should target specific sectors of society.
  D practical help with financial planning is more useful than formal instruction.

36 From the final paragraph, we understand that the charitable foundation
  A has already gained broad support across the financial sector.
  B has plans to set up parallel schemes in a range of communities.
  C has secured sufficient funding to produce some audio-visual resources.
  D has agreed to work with partner organisations that have compatible aims.

Part 6

You are going to read four reviews of a book about swimming. For questions **37–40**, choose from the reviewers **A–D**. The reviewers may be chosen more than once.
Mark your answers **on the separate answer sheet**.

Why We Swim by Bonnie Tsui

A Bonnie Tsui is a passionate advocate of swimming lessons for all. In *Why We Swim*, she recounts the myriad ways humans have interacted with water over thousands of years. At the heart of the book are extraordinary tales of long-distance swimmers and what drives them. Take Gudlaugur Fridthorsson, who in 1984 swam for six hours through freezing water after his fishing boat sank. His adventure was widely reported by the media, with the focus largely on his physical traits. Tsui, however, takes a refreshingly different approach, insisting it was resilience, a quality created by his Icelandic upbringing, that kept him alive. Her book is also a persuasive contemplation on swimming's transformative effects on the mind, something regular swimmers like myself can attest to. But it's the elements of memoir that make this book stand out, with Tsui describing her lifelong connection with the ocean and all that swimming has taught her.

B Bonnie Tsui is hooked on swimming and believes everyone has the right to learn. The passages in *Why We Swim* in which Tsui claims that swimming can alter people's emotional state and the way they perceive the world left me unconvinced, perhaps because I'm a non-swimmer. But the descriptions of intimate moments such as how a love of swimming helped her reunite with her father are memorable and endearing. Also behind the book's success are the inspiring tales of swimmers like Gudlaugur Fridthorsson. Through her conversations with him, Tsui comes to realise that his being an Icelander was key to his survival in an ice-cold ocean, an aspect of the narrative previously overlooked, and which readers will appreciate. Tsui's discussion with a palaeontologist about Neolithic paintings of swimmers is likewise fascinating, although the paintings themselves say little about our ancestors' attitude to swimming – whether it was practised out of necessity or pleasure.

C The first-known depictions of swimming are on the walls of a Saharan cave, drawn way back when there were lakes in the area – evidence that humans have always enjoyed this activity. But according to Bonnie Tsui in *Why We Swim*, swimming promotes well-being too, and for her, has even helped resolve personal issues, though whether this is the case for all swimmers is debatable. Swimming is also essential to survival, as with Icelandic fisherman Gudlaugur Fridthorsson, who endured six hours in the 5°C sea. Considering that this remarkable story has already received extensive coverage, and that Tsui adds little to it, she should perhaps have opted for a lower-profile subject. Readers will, however, be taken aback by the shameful history of public pools in the US, which could only be used by the privileged few. Still today, it is to our discredit that socio-economics dictates whether a pool is accessible to a community or whether swimming is on the curriculum.

D In *Why We Swim*, Bonnie Tsui describes the deep bonds she's forged with other swimmers, and why people become obsessed with swimming. She is also aware that unaffordable entry fees to swimming facilities mean that some children, and adults even, will never become comfortable in the water, and she rightly condemns this situation. She praises the Icelandic tradition of subsidized public pools, and actually interviews Gudlaugur Fridthorsson – the shipwrecked Icelander that survived the frigid North Atlantic Ocean. It's to Tsui's credit that instead of merely revisiting his story, she chooses to emphasize the link between his cultural heritage and sheer determination to swim back to land. There is archaeology in this book too. Tsui explains how primitive drawings provide proof that we have been swimming for millennia. As true as that may be, we still cannot infer from these what original motivation people had for developing this skill.

Which reviewer

shares an opinion with D regarding the opportunities to swim that ordinary people have?	**37**
has a different opinion from the others on whether Tsui explored Gudlaugur Fridthorsson's ordeal in an original way?	**38**
shares an opinion with D on what prehistoric images of swimmers are able to reveal?	**39**
expresses a different opinion from B on the psychological effects of swimming?	**40**

Part 7

You are going to read an article about how science is reported in the media. Six paragraphs have been removed from the article. Choose from the paragraphs **A–G** the one which fits each gap (**41–46**). There is one extra paragraph which you do not need to use.

Mark your answers **on the separate answer sheet**.

What chocolate and Nobel Prizes reveal about our trust in scientists

Wouldn't it be great if chocolate were good for you? It's no wonder many news outlets leap on research that appears to show potential benefits to eating it. But the history of such coverage provides a cautionary tale about why we should be wary of scientists' claims that are reported in the media, as well as the way the stories are framed by journalists. In 2012, for example, Dr Franz Messerli published a short article in the prestigious *New England Journal of Medicine* that looked at a range of recent studies into the cognitive impact of chocolate consumption.

> **41**

In his article, Messerli suggested there was a clear link between the average amount of chocolate eaten in a country and the number of Nobel Prize winners it produced, relative to population size. He proposed that to enhance cognitive abilities (and consequently its number of Nobel Prizes), each country should radically increase its chocolate intake.

> **42**

As a result, news reports about the intellectual benefits of eating chocolate flooded screens and newspapers. Journalists had taken the fact that the article was published in a respected journal as a guarantee of quality, little realising that it had been placed in a section called 'Occasional Notes', earmarked for jovial contributions such as Messerli's. Meanwhile, fellow scientists were outraged. Why would the *New England Journal of Medicine* disseminate such a thing?

> **43**

Despite the apparent ease with which Messerli's assertions were thus disproved, since the release of his article many serious papers and earnest letters have been published on the subject. What's more, traditional and social media have continuously covered the story, mostly without critical reflection, perpetuating the idea that there might be a link between chocolate and national brainpower.

> **44**

When claims made in articles aimed at the general public are subsequently disproved, for example, the public loses trust in both researchers and journalists. Because research papers are rarely page-turners or accessible to non-specialists, we typically rely on reporters to make sense of new findings. But while many news outlets report on research, few have dedicated journalists with the skills, expertise and experience to cast a sufficiently critical eye over dubious or difficult-to-interpret results.

> **45**

But is the media totally to blame for the attention-grabbing yet flawed reporting that this exemplifies? Though some journalists need to better explain research, scientists too play a role in transmitting the information, and unfortunately, they often do not try to correct misunderstandings. For example, in the case of the chocolate-Nobel story, the scientists involved did little to address the confusion engulfing the mass media.

> **46**

In contrast, when scientists participate wholeheartedly in publicising their findings, it can have real impact. For instance, in 2015, US journalists reported that over 80% of pupils at kindergarten in one area were not vaccinated against diseases including polio and measles. Scientists looked into these vaccine refusals, and an information campaign was mounted. By involving the community and rebuilding trust, immunisation rates improved radically. The chocolate-Nobel debacle has taught us that all scientific publications can be misinterpreted. Scientists must therefore recognise their responsibility towards promoting a general understanding of science. No one should have to base their opinions on attractive but inaccurate soundbites, no matter how tasty they seem.

A Hence a story about scientists' latest failure to find an explanation for why antimatter didn't destroy the universe at its creation led to the misleading headline: '"It should NOT EXIST" … scientists fear universe could DIE at any moment'.

B This unusual proposition, however, was meant as nothing more than a droll story, a friendly reminder to colleagues that over-interpreting correlations can lead to incorrect claims. Unfortunately, few people understood that the 'research' was actually a joke.

C But somehow, this study was sensationalised in the media as ground-breaking research proving that a popular foodstuff would protect against a serious disease. Once again, the misinterpretation was not corrected.

D Regrettably, this amusing anecdote is far from an isolated incident. Much coverage of science is flawed at best and downright wrong at worst. This is important because scientific misinformation can have adverse effects on individual and societal behaviour.

E Undertaking this type of research seemed to make sense, superficially at least. After all, flavanols, one of the many compounds present in this ever-popular treat, are thought to facilitate brain cell connections and thereby boost thinking skills.

F In fact, studies have shown that a similar lack of communication by researchers, and their reluctance to engage with the public, both contribute to this kind of inaccurate reporting on research. This inevitably leaves the wider population more open to half-truths and misinformation.

G Several immediately and aggressively contested the notion that binge-eating chocolate would increase the number of Nobel laureates. They highlighted the absurdity of the claim by pointing out that there was also an astonishingly high correlation between the number of IKEA furniture stores in a country and Nobel Prize laureates.

Part 8

You are going to read an extract from a memoir of a dancer. For questions **47–56**, choose from the sections (**A–D**). The sections may be chosen more than once.
Mark your answers **on the separate answer sheet**.

In which section does the writer

compare the way certain people evaluated the dancing of others?	**47**
claim she found discussing dance more interesting than her contemporaries did?	**48**
describe the physical discomfort she experienced as a result of a particular activity?	**49**
explain how watching other people dancing influenced her own dance?	**50**
outline the impact that an early review had on her career?	**51**
express admiration for a specific person whose approach she wished to replicate?	**52**
refer to disliking a certain technique used by one of her teachers?	**53**
highlight the importance of particular language when describing dance?	**54**
mention being unsure about which form of dance she was best suited to?	**55**
recall how wanting to dance brought her into conflict with someone else?	**56**

Through the eyes of a dancer

Wendy Perron describes her career as a dancer and dance critic

A   The year I started kindergarten, my mother opened a school of creative dance in our basement in New Jersey. Looking back on that moment, I realise she was laying the foundation for my life. When I was seven, I began weekly ballet lessons with a former dancer of the Ballets Russes, who pounded a stick on the floor to keep time, which didn't exactly foster joy in executing the steps. But that didn't put me off and during my last two years of high school, I decided to enrol at the Martha Graham School of Contemporary Dance. For me, modern dance and ballet seemed like different planets, and for years I struggled to figure out which one I belonged to, before ultimately settling on the latter. I worked tirelessly in all these classes, but at the same time I also observed fellow dancers. I analyzed and attempted to reproduce the style of those I most wished to emulate, at the same time appreciating how much pain they go through to achieve it.

B   After high school, I enrolled to study dance and psychology at the liberal arts college Bennington, where one of my teachers was literary critic Stanley Edgar Hyman. He liked what I wrote but I always found completing assignments an ordeal, necessitating many hours burning the midnight oil, searching for the right combinations of words. Soon I was chomping at the bit to drop out of college and go dance in New York full-time. I remember a long and heated phone call with my mother by the end of which I had reluctantly agreed to stay on. During my last year I choreographed a lot, including a solo that I later performed at Dance Theater Workshop. Deborah Jowitt, one of the founders of DTW, assessed my solo for the *Village Voice*, saying my dance had a 'blazing purity'. I was off and running as a downtown dancer and choreographer! Around the same time, I noticed I was more involved than my peers in talking about the dances I had seen and that I kept these conversations going long after they had switched off.

C   So when Deborah Jowitt and her colleague Marcia Siegel offered a course in dance criticism at Dance Theater Workshop, I signed up. The attraction was less that I would learn how to write texts like critiques, and more that I wanted and needed to talk about dance. We would write articles and then read them aloud to develop an ear for rhythm. Writing about dance demands imagination: you not only walk, run and leap; you glide, spring, curve, stagger, float and entwine. I've been searching to get it right ever since. In that course we debated questions like, *What is a critic's job?* Deborah and Marcia were very different types of writer. Description, for Deborah, required objective analysis, whereas for Marcia it led to sharp opinions. I never really decided what sort of critic I was.

D   My first assignment was to review a new group of college dancers called Pilobolus. But I don't think my comments were particularly insightful or well-constructed. It was later, at the *SoHo News*, that I found my groove; I felt I could bring readers into the world I had just seen. But when I started getting more offers to write than to choreograph, I backed off. Anyway, sitting at a typewriter was bad for my back and I was already, in my twenties, getting spasms it took days to recover from. One of my heroes at the time was Susan Sontag for forging new ways to write about art. She argued that when critiquing any artwork, you had to sense it, pick up clues from it, not analyze it. Her philosophy fit the new kinds of dance that were then exploding into view, and I've tried to follow it ever since.

WRITING (1 hour 30 minutes)

Part 1

You **must** answer this question. Write your answer in **220–260** words in an appropriate style **on the separate answer sheet**.

---

1 Your class has taken part in an online discussion about the reasons why working in teams is useful. You have made the notes below:

> ### Reasons why working in teams is useful:
> * sociable
> * efficient
> * creative

> **Some opinions expressed in the discussion:**
>
> "I enjoy getting together with the team."
>
> "We waste less time."
>
> "As a team, we come up with some great ideas."

Write an essay for your tutor discussing **two** of the reasons in your notes about why working in teams is useful. You should **explain which reason you think is more useful** and **justify** your choice.

You may, if you wish, make use of the opinions expressed in the discussion, but you should use your own words as far as possible.

Part 2

Write an answer to **one** of the questions **2–4** in this part. Write your answer in **220–260** words in an appropriate style **on the separate answer sheet**. Put the question number in the box at the top of the page.

---

2   The college where you study is planning to celebrate its 100th anniversary. The college principal has asked for ideas of what the celebrations could include. You have decided to email the principal to suggest inviting a guest speaker.

You should explain why a guest speaker would be a good way to open the celebrations, describe the qualities that make a good guest speaker and recommend someone you think would be ideal for the role.

Write your **email** to the college principal.

3   You see this announcement on a health and fitness website:

> **Health and Fitness Apps**
>
> Do you use an app to keep fit and healthy? If so, why not write a review of it for our website?
>
> Briefly describe the app and say how effective it is. Also, explain who you think would benefit from using it, and how it could be improved.
>
> Reviews will be published next month!

Write your **review**.

4   You see this notice in your college online newsletter:

> **Student clubs**
>
> If you are interested in starting a student club this year, please submit your ideas to the college principal for approval.

You have decided you want to start a new student club. You should write a proposal, outlining what type of club you want to set up, describing the aims of the club and explaining its benefits.

Write your **proposal**.

LISTENING (approximately 40 minutes)

Part 1

You will hear three different extracts. For questions **1–6**, choose the answer (**A, B** or **C**) which fits best according to what you hear. There are two questions for each extract.

Listening test audio

Extract One

You hear two psychologists discussing problems people have with concentration.

1 When talking about concentration, the woman is

   A describing how she has changed her own approach to it.

   B comparing problems people have now and in the past.

   C identifying why it's difficult to maintain it.

2 What do they agree about one technique intended to improve concentration for busy people?

   A It's often misunderstood.

   B It takes time to perfect.

   C It works better in some businesses than others.

Extract Two

You hear part of an interview with a man who writes stories that are then turned into graphic novels, books in which the plot is mainly conveyed through pictures.

3 When asked about collaborating with artists, the man

   A identifies ways of choosing those he wants to work with.

   B outlines the approach he takes when working with them.

   C describes positive experiences he has had working with them.

4 What does the man think about experimenting with different genres of graphic novel?

   A He knows exploring other genres is necessary for his creative development.

   B He finds the notion of competing against writers of other genres exciting.

   C He understands that adapting to an unfamiliar genre can be challenging.

Extract Three

You hear part of a discussion programme about predicting the future.

5   What does the woman think can help people predict the future accurately?

   A the ability to spot certain patterns

   B thorough investigations

   C being lucky when making guesses

6   The man reveals he often gets things wrong when predicting the future because he

   A fails to consider long-term rewards.

   B deliberately ignores important issues.

   C tends to be too optimistic.

Part 2

You will hear a man called Leo Mitchell giving a talk to a group of university students about volunteering for a conservation organisation in Bali, an Indonesian island. For questions **7–14**, complete the sentences with a word or short phrase.

Listening test audio

Volunteering for a conservation organisation in Bali

Leo recommends gaining a **(7)** .... before going to Bali.

Leo explains that years of **(8)** .... during the first half of the last century

damaged the coral reefs in the area of Bali where his organisation is based.

Leo says that a **(9)** .... is the most important element in the design of

an artificial reef.

Leo and his colleagues are currently assessing the level of

(10) .... to see what effect their organisation is having.

Volunteers are also needed to work in a **(11)** ....

which Leo's organisation helped to set up.

Used plastic is now cut up and turned into **(12)** .... , which are in

high demand.

A recently introduced task for Leo's organisation is the **(13)** .... of

turtle eggs.

Leo thinks the word **(14)** .... accurately describes the hours that

volunteers should expect to work.

Part 3

You will hear an interview in which two film critics, Julie Bahn and Amit Ray, talk about their careers. For questions **15–20**, choose the answer (**A, B, C** or **D**) which fits best according to what you hear.

Listening test audio

15 Julie says that her choice of career
   A was a reflection of her childhood interests.
   B was influenced by her college environment.
   C was made due to her natural talent for writing.
   D was the result of an assignment she had as a student.

16 What does Amit say about having a career as a film critic?
   A He has never taken it seriously, despite his success.
   B He saw it as an opportunity to be involved in the movie industry.
   C He thought it was suitable for someone needing an intellectual challenge.
   D He only pursued it because of the industry contacts he already had.

17 How did Julie overcome a challenging part of her job?
   A She became more honest about the films she was reviewing.
   B She learnt how to deal with difficult interviewees.
   C She focused on under-reported aspects of the film business.
   D She used contacts to her advantage.

18 Amit admits that during a typical working day
   A he has problems concentrating on what he is doing.
   B he has to spend a lot of time planning his work schedule.
   C he needs to take breaks outdoors on a regular basis.
   D he likes to have a number of projects to move between.

19 What do Amit and Julie agree about being a good film critic?
   A The necessary skill can be acquired online.
   B Having a broad understanding of the medium is essential.
   C There is no substitute to viewing as many films as possible.
   D It is vital to be well read in all genres of art and culture.

20 What advice does Amit have for anyone thinking of becoming a film critic?
   A They must be willing to work for a number of media outlets.
   B They will find that it is unlikely to remain a viable career for much longer.
   C They need to keep up to date with technological changes in the media.
   D They could try to increase their own media presence to begin with.

Part 4

You will hear five short extracts in which people are talking about working in offices.

Listening test audio

TASK ONE

For questions **21–25**, choose from the list (**A–H**) what each person says they have gained from working in their office.

TASK TWO

For questions **26–30**, choose from the list (**A–H**) what advice each person gives about starting work in their office.

While you listen, you must complete both tasks.

TASK ONE		TASK TWO	
A an ability to multi-task		**A** impress your boss	
B an appreciation of interpersonal skills	Speaker 1 [ ] [21]	**B** never gossip	Speaker 1 [ ] [26]
C an openness to learning	Speaker 2 [ ] [22]	**C** move around regularly	Speaker 2 [ ] [27]
D tolerance of others' weaknesses	Speaker 3 [ ] [23]	**D** consult others	Speaker 3 [ ] [28]
E advanced IT skills	Speaker 4 [ ] [24]	**E** dress smartly	Speaker 4 [ ] [29]
F increased confidence	Speaker 5 [ ] [25]	**F** avoid disturbing people	Speaker 5 [ ] [30]
G greater self-knowledge		**G** consider others' views	
H time management skills		**H** socialise with colleagues	

53114

OFFICE USE ONLY - DO NOT WRITE OR MAKE ANY MARK ABOVE THIS LINE   Page 1 of 2

CAMBRIDGE
English

Candidate Name		Candidate Number	
Centre Name		Centre Number	
Examination Title		Examination Details	
Candidate Signature		Assessment Date	

Supervisor: If the candidate is ABSENT or has WITHDRAWN shade here ○

Advanced Reading and Use of English Candidate Answer

Part 1

	A	B	C	D
1	○	○	○	○
2	○	○	○	○
3	○	○	○	○
4	○	○	○	○
5	○	○	○	○
6	○	○	○	○
7	○	○	○	○
8	○	○	○	○

Instructions
Use a PENCIL (B or HB).
Rub out any answer you want to change using an eraser.

Parts 1, 5, 6, 7 and 8:
Mark ONE letter for each question.
For example, if you think A is the right answer to the question, mark your answer sheet like this:

0 A ● C

Parts 2, 3 and 4: Write your answer clearly in CAPITAL LETTERS.

For parts 2 and 3, write one letter in each box.

0 EXAMPLE

Part 2

		Do not write below here
9		9 1 ○ 0 ○
10		10 1 ○ 0 ○
11		11 1 ○ 0 ○
12		12 1 ○ 0 ○
13		13 1 ○ 0 ○
14		14 1 ○ 0 ○
15		15 1 ○ 0 ○
16		16 1 ○ 0 ○ **Continues over** ➡

OFFICE USE ONLY - DO NOT WRITE OR MAKE ANY MARK BELOW THIS LINE   Page 1 of 2

53114

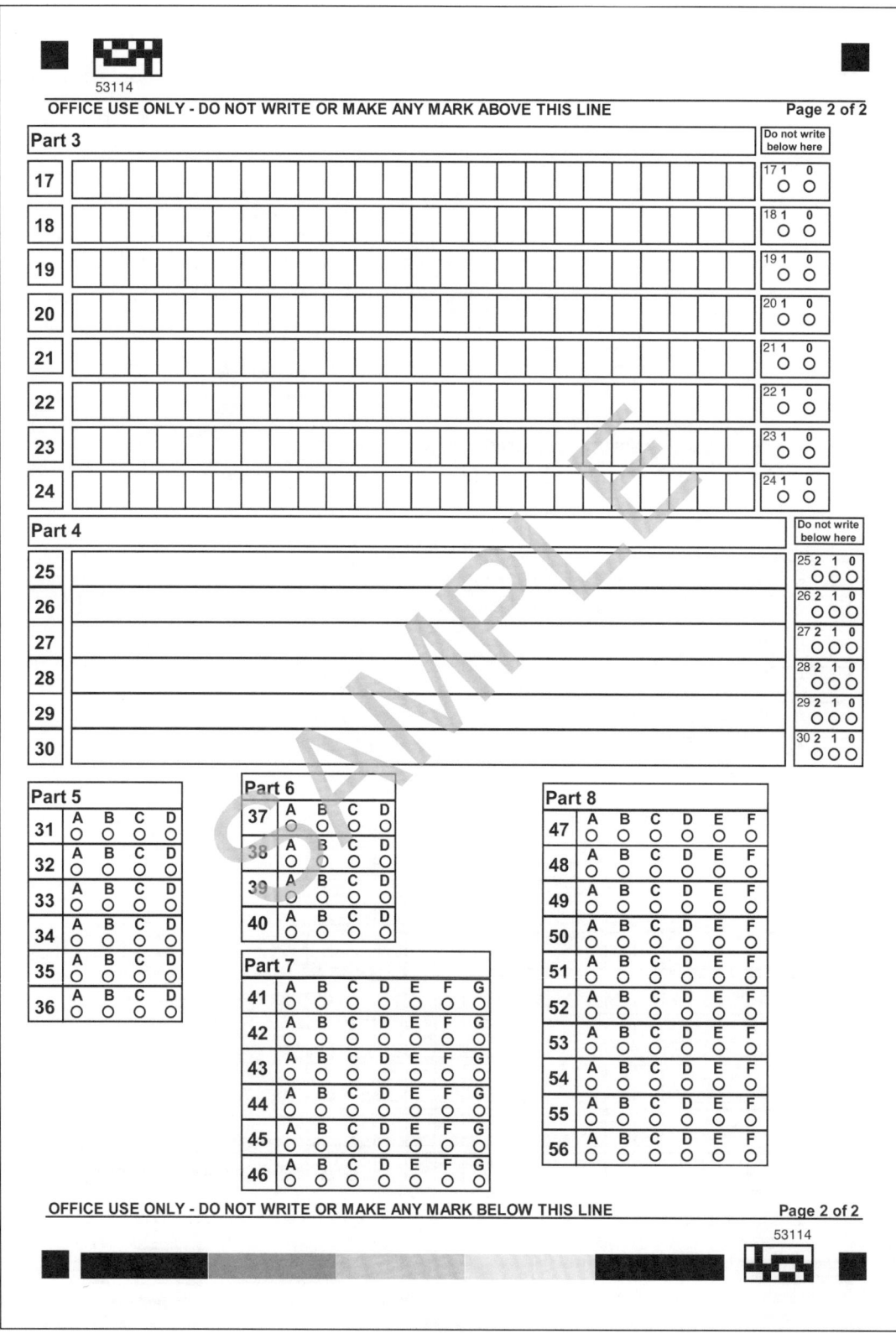

1036

OFFICE USE ONLY - DO NOT WRITE OR MAKE ANY MARK ABOVE THIS LINE   Page 1 of 2

CAMBRIDGE
English

Candidate Name		Candidate Number	

Centre Name		Centre Number	

Examination Title		Examination Details	

Candidate Signature		Assessment Date	

Supervisor: If the candidate is ABSENT or has WITHDRAWN shade here ○

Advanced Listening Candidate Answer Sheet

Instructions
Use a PENCIL (B or HB).
Rub out any answer you want to change using an eraser.

Parts 1, 3 and 4:
Mark ONE letter for each question.

For example, if you think **A** is the right answer to the question, mark your answer sheet like this:

Part 2:
Write your answer clearly in CAPITAL LETTERS.

Write one letter or number in each box.
If the answer has more than one word, leave one box empty between words.

For example:

0 | NUMBER | 12

Turn this sheet over to start

OFFICE USE ONLY - DO NOT WRITE OR MAKE ANY MARK BELOW THIS LINE   Page 1 of 2

1036

Sample answer sheet: Listening

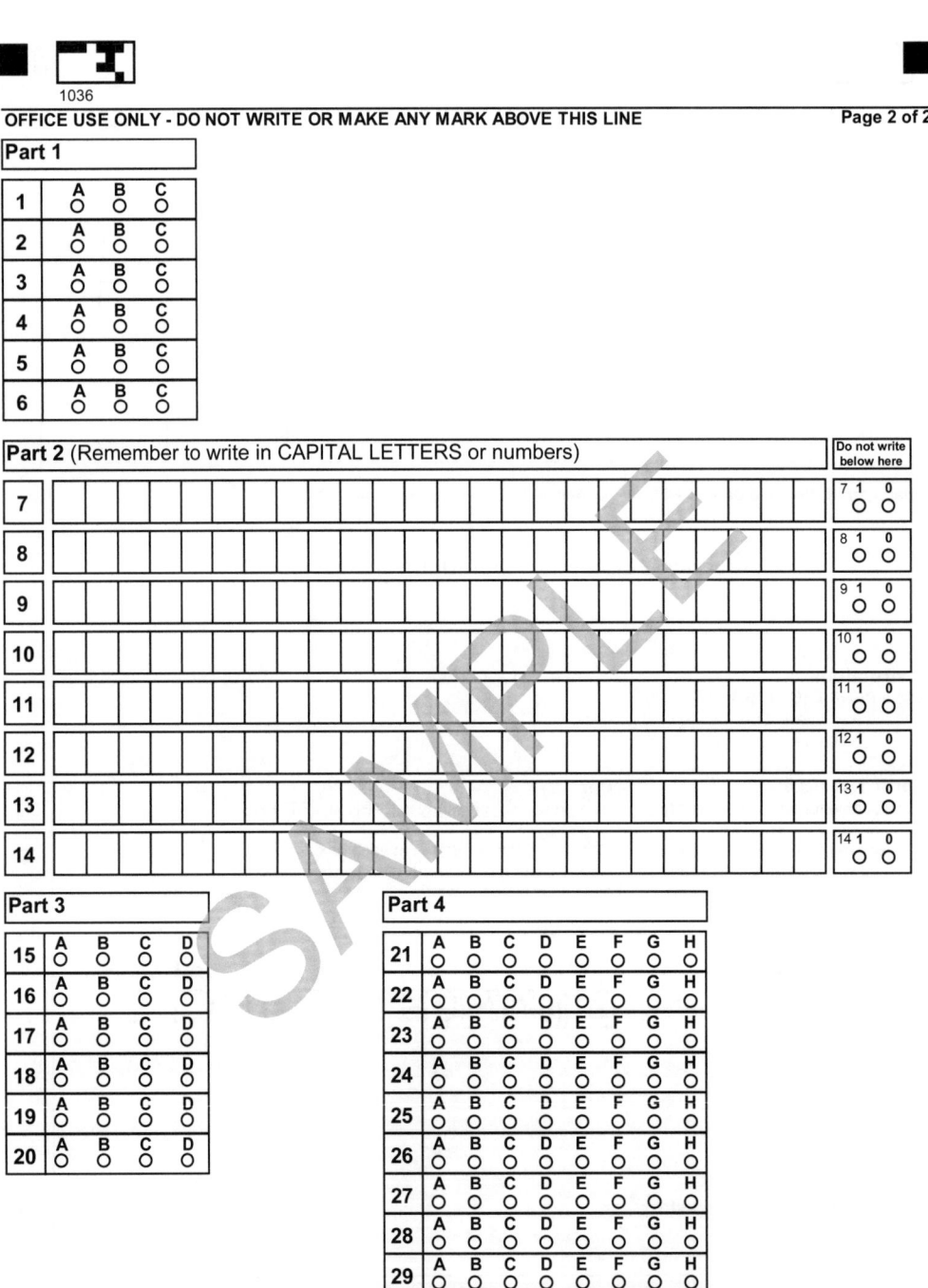

1036

Part 1

	A	B	C
1	○	○	○
2	○	○	○
3	○	○	○
4	○	○	○
5	○	○	○
6	○	○	○

Part 2 (Remember to write in CAPITAL LETTERS or numbers)

Do not write below here

		1 0
7		7 ○ ○
8		8 ○ ○
9		9 ○ ○
10		10 ○ ○
11		11 ○ ○
12		12 ○ ○
13		13 ○ ○
14		14 ○ ○

Part 3

	A	B	C	D
15	○	○	○	○
16	○	○	○	○
17	○	○	○	○
18	○	○	○	○
19	○	○	○	○
20	○	○	○	○

Part 4

	A	B	C	D	E	F	G	H
21	○	○	○	○	○	○	○	○
22	○	○	○	○	○	○	○	○
23	○	○	○	○	○	○	○	○
24	○	○	○	○	○	○	○	○
25	○	○	○	○	○	○	○	○
26	○	○	○	○	○	○	○	○
27	○	○	○	○	○	○	○	○
28	○	○	○	○	○	○	○	○
29	○	○	○	○	○	○	○	○
30	○	○	○	○	○	○	○	○

1036

Acknowledgements

The authors and publishers acknowledge the following sources of copyright material and are grateful for the permissions granted. While every effort has been made, it has not always been possible to identify the sources of all the material used, or to trace all copyright holders. If any omissions are brought to our notice, we will be happy to include the appropriate acknowledgements on reprinting and in the next update to the digital edition, as applicable.

Key: L = Listening, RUE = Reading and Use of English, S = Speaking.

Text

L4: The Interview portal for the adapted text from 'Film Critic Interview', *The Interview portal*, 10.06.2020. Copyright © 2020 Offbeat, unusual, unconventional & interesting career interviews. Reproduced with kind permission; **RUE1:** Nick D'Aloisio for the text about Nick D'Aloisio. Copyright © Nick D'Aloisio. Reproduced with kind permission; Condé Nast for the adapted text from 'Inky the Octopus and the Upsides of Anthropomorphism' by Rachel Riederer, *The New Yorker*, 26.04.2016. Copyright © 2016 Condé Nast. Reproduced with permission; Karen Harris for the adapted text from 'Scholarly sources versus popular' by Karen Harris, *THE – Times Higher Education*, 20.03.2014. Copyright © 2014 Karen Harris. Reproduced with kind permission; **RUE2:** The Guardian for the adapted text from 'Rain is sizzling bacon, cars are lions roaring: the art of sound in movies' by Jordan Kisner, *The Guardian*, 22.07.2015. Copyright © 2015 Guardian News & Media Limited. Reproduced with permission; The Financial Times Ltd for the adapted text from 'Unlocking the World' by John Darwin, *The Financial Times Ltd*, 02.11.2020. Copyright © 2020 The Financial Times Ltd. All Rights Reserved. Reproduced with permission; The Guardian for the adapted text from 'The nose has it: it's no surprise humans' sense of smell can be as good as dogs' by Sarah McCartney, *The Guardian*, 15.05.2017. Copyright © 2017 Guardian News & Media Limited. Reproduced with permission; American Institute of Physics for the adapted text from 'Oil Rigs May Get Second Lives as Fish Habitat' by Katharine Gammon, *Inside Science,* 04.06.2019. Copyright © 2019 American Institute of Physics. Reproduced with permission; **RUE3:** The Independent for the adapted text from 'Pterosaurs: Winged-reptiles gradually improved flying ability over millions of years, study finds' by Conrad Duncan, *The Independent*, 28.10.2020. Copyright © 2020 Independent Digital News & Media Ltd. Reproduced with permission; The Guardian for the adapted text from 'The museum of everything: do you have time to look at 150,000 exhibits?' by Andrew Dickson, *The Guardian*, 21.09.2020. Copyright © 2020 Guardian News & Media Limited. Reproduced with permission; The Guardian for the adapted text from 'In dialogue with Mozart: composer's violin brought back to life' by Kate Connolly, *The Guardian*, 09.10.2020. Copyright © 2020 Guardian News & Media Limited. Reproduced with permission; CR Fashion Book for the adapted text from 'How Velcro Forever Changed Fashion' by Andrea Cheng, *CR Fashion Book*, 10.04.2019. Copyright © 2019 CR Fashion Book. Reproduced with kind permission; **RUE4:** Evening Standard Ltd for the adapted text from 'Grandmother's tiger sculpture sparks armed police and helicopter response' by Rebecca Speare-Cole, *Evening Standard Ltd*, 04.05.2020. Copyright © 2020 Evening Standard Ltd. Reproduced with permission; The Financial Times Ltd for the adapted text from 'Why financial literacy matters more than ever' by Patrick Jenkins, *The Financial Times Ltd*, 19.11.2020. Copyright © 2020 The Financial Times Ltd. All Rights Reserved. Reproduced with permission; Katrine K. Donois for the adapted text from 'What a link between chocolate and Nobel prizes reveals about our trust in scientists' by Katrine K. Donois, *The Conversation*, 29.10.2020. Copyright © 2020 Katrine K. Donois. Reproduced with kind permission; Wesleyan University Press for the adapted text from 'Dance Memoir' in *Through the Eyes of a Dancer* by Wendy Perron. Copyright © 2013 by Wesleyan University Press. Reproduced with permission.

Acknowledgements

Photography
The following photographs are sourced from Getty Images:

S1: XiXinXing; Maskot; Alistair Berg/DigitalVision; hadynyah/iStock/Getty Images Plus; AzmanJaka/E+; Caiaimage/Sam Edwards/iStock/Getty Images Plus; **S4:** Sorapop/iStock/Getty Images Plus.

The following photographs are sourced from another library:

S2: Tetra Images, LLC/Alamy Stock Photo; LightField Studios Inc./Alamy Stock Photo; Cavan Images/Alamy Stock Photo; Arterra Picture Library/Alamy Stock Photo; Volodymyr Tverdokhlib/Alamy Stock Photo; **S3:** MBI/Alamy Stock Photo; David Gee/Alamy Stock Photo; Bax Walker/Alamy Stock Photo; Prostock-studio/Alamy Stock Photo; Reinhard Dirscherl/Alamy Stock Photo; Pablo Sarompas/Alamy Stock Photo; **S4:** Dash/Alamy Stock Photo; Wiskerke/Alamy Stock Photo; Gina Kelly/Alamy Stock Photo; Westend61 GmbH/Alamy Stock Photo; Andrey Armyagov/Alamy Stock Photo.

Illustrations
Cambridge University Press & Assessment.

Audio
Audio production by dsound recording Ltd.

Typesetting
Typeset by QBS Learning.

Visual materials for the Speaking test

- What might the people be discussing?
- What might happen next?

1A

1B

1C

Visual materials for the Speaking test

- Why might the screens be important to the people in these situations?
- How easy might it be for the people to manage without the screens?

1D

1E

1F

1G

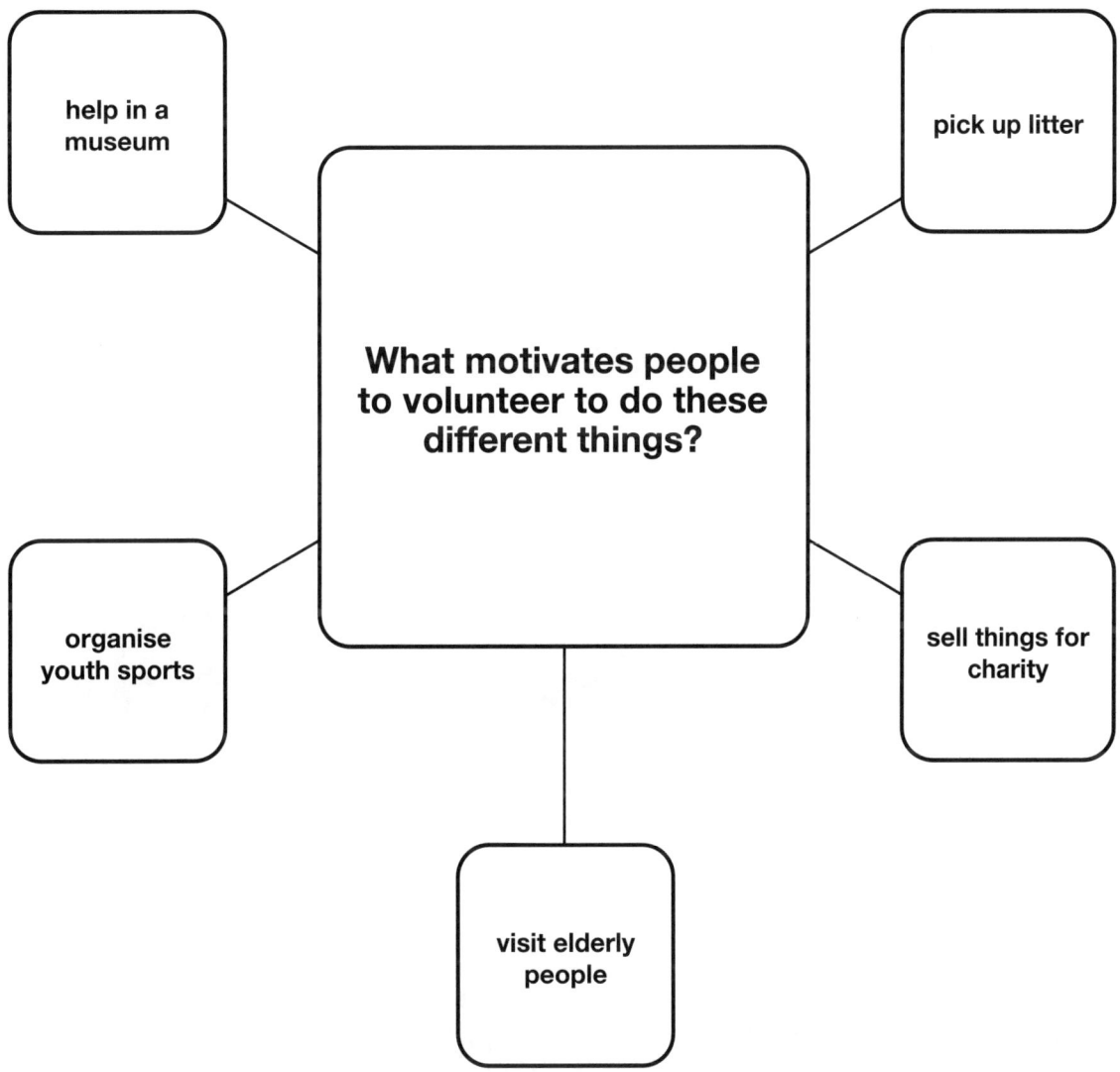

help in a museum

pick up litter

What motivates people to volunteer to do these different things?

organise youth sports

sell things for charity

visit elderly people

- Why might the people find using wood satisfying in these situations?
- How skilled might they need to be?

2A

2B

2C

- Why might the plants be important to the people in these situations?
- How might the people be feeling?

2D

2E

2F

2G

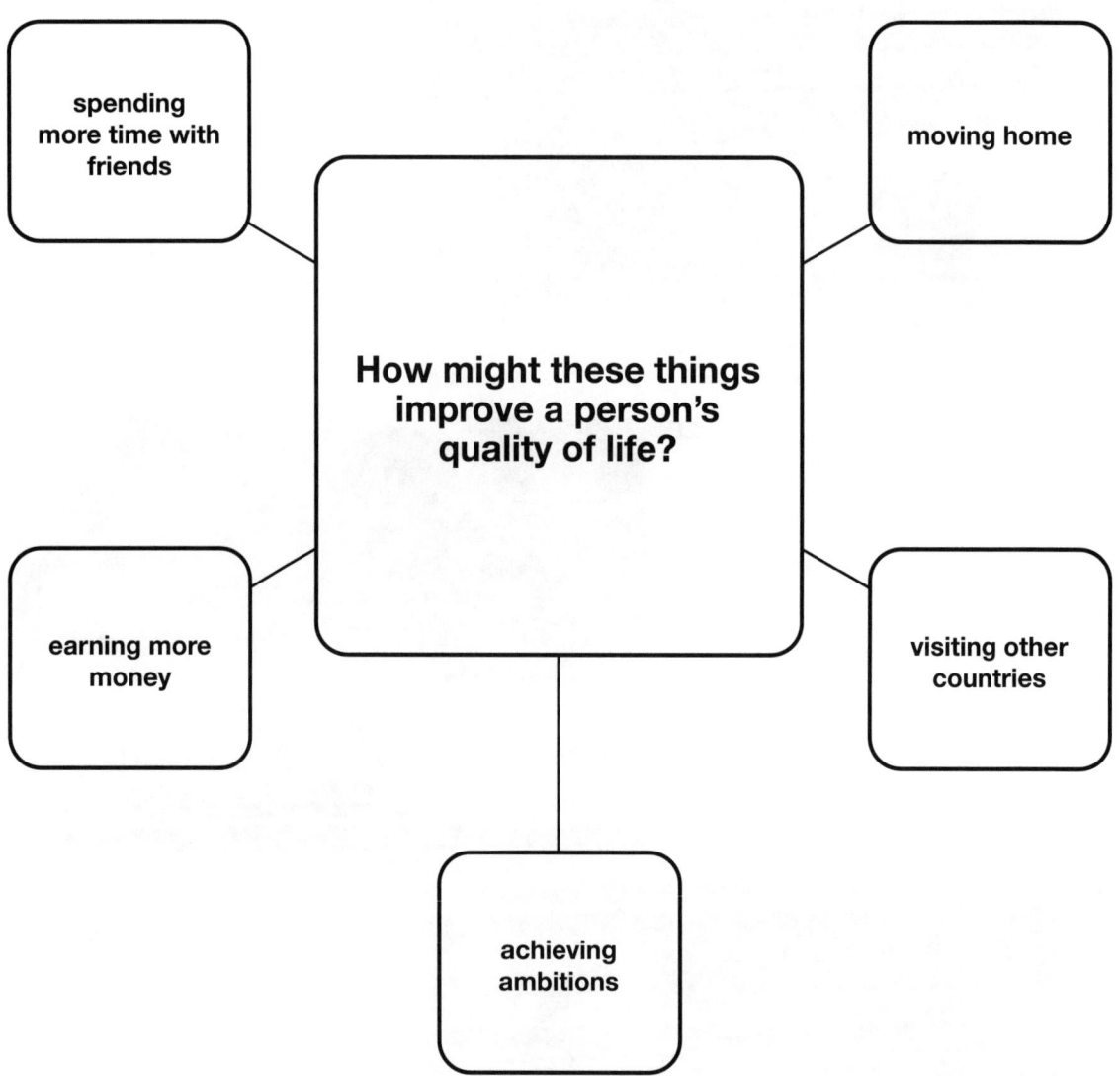

spending more time with friends

moving home

How might these things improve a person's quality of life?

earning more money

visiting other countries

achieving ambitions

- What might have caused the situation?
- What might happen next?

3A

3B

3C

- Why might people be using light in these situations?
- What difference might it make if they didn't have it?

3D

3E

3F

3G

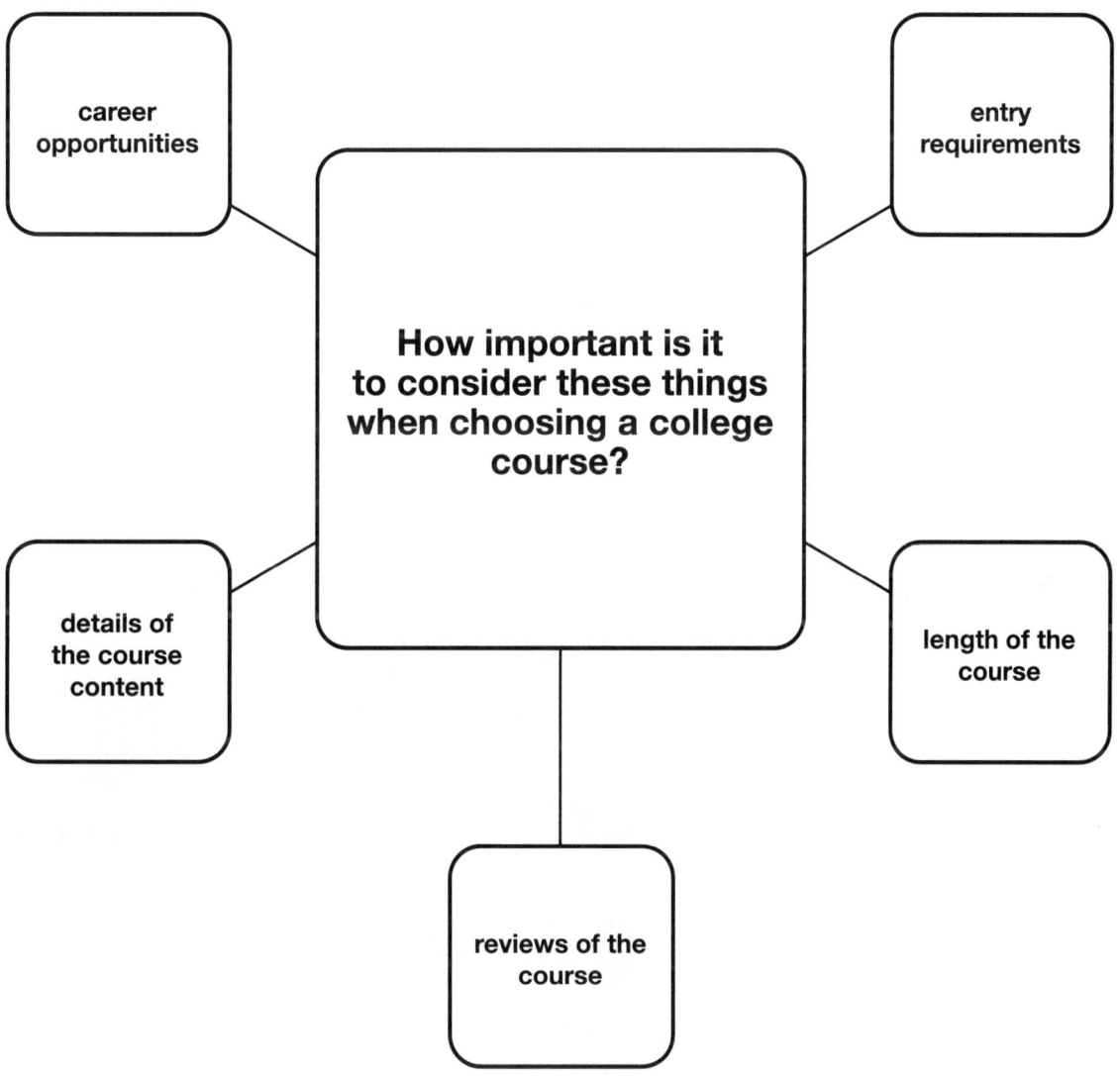

career opportunities

entry requirements

How important is it to consider these things when choosing a college course?

details of the course content

length of the course

reviews of the course

Visual materials for the Speaking test

- Why might the people be taking photographs in these situations?
- How important might the quality of the photograph be?

4A

4B

4C

- What might the people be thinking about while doing activities alone?
- How different might the experience be with other people?

4D

4E

4F

4G

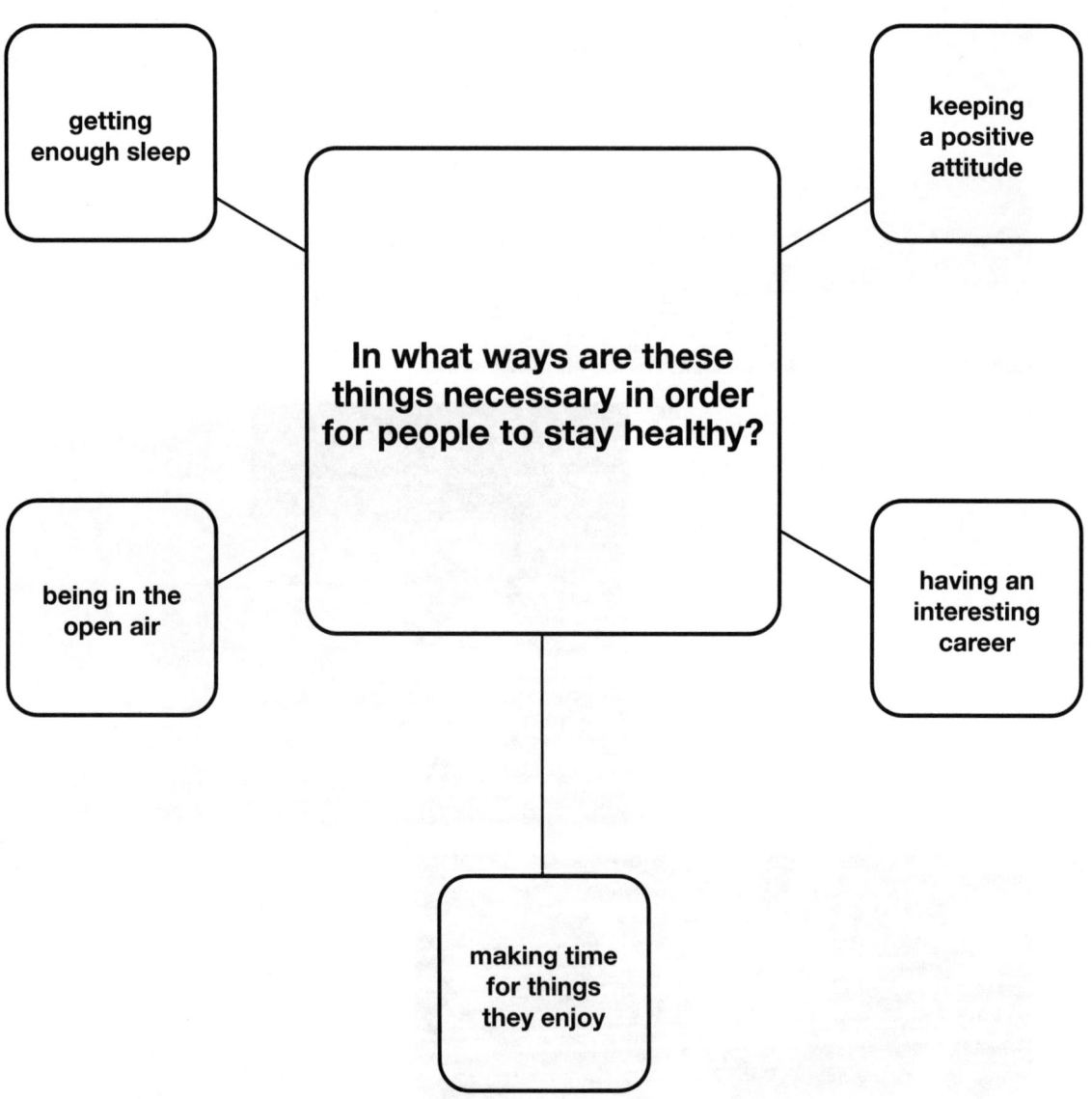

getting enough sleep

keeping a positive attitude

In what ways are these things necessary in order for people to stay healthy?

being in the open air

having an interesting career

making time for things they enjoy